The **SMART NEW WAY** to **GET HIRED**

USE EMOTIONAL INTELLIGENCE AND LAND THE RIGHT JOB

LISA CALDAS KAPPESSER

With a Foreword by Steven J. Stein, Ph.D., author of
Emotional Intelligence for Dummies and coauthor of
The EQ Edge: Emotional Intelligence and Your Success

jist Works
America's Career Publisher®

THE SMART NEW WAY TO GET HIRED
USE EMOTIONAL INTELLIGENCE AND LAND THE RIGHT JOB

© 2010 by Lisa Caldas Kappesser

Published by JIST Works, an imprint of JIST Publishing
7321 Shadeland Station, Suite 200
Indianapolis, IN 46256-3923
Phone: 800-648-JIST   Fax: 877-454-7839   E-mail: info@jist.com

Visit our Web site at **www.jist.com** for information on JIST, free job search tips, tables of contents, sample pages, and ordering instructions for our many products!

Quantity discounts are available for JIST products. Please call our Sales Department at 800-648-5478 for a free catalog and more information.

Acquisitions Editor: Susan Pines
Development Editor: Heather Stith
Interior Designer and Page Layout: Aleata Halbig
Cover Designer: Amy Peppler Adams
Proofreader: Jeanne Clark
Indexer: Kelly D. Henthorne

Printed in the United States of America
14 13 12 11 10 09   9 8 7 6 5 4 3 2 1

    Library of Congress Cataloging-in-Publication Data
Kappesser, Lisa Caldas, 1961-
   The smart new way to get hired : use emotional intelligence and land the right job / Lisa Caldas Kappesser.
        p. cm.
   Includes bibliographical references and index.
   ISBN 978-1-59357-664-6 (alk. paper)
   1. Job hunting--Psychological aspects. 2. Career development--Psychological aspects. 3. Emotional intelligence. I. Title.
   HF5382.7.K368 2010
   650.14--dc22
                                        2009043790

We have been careful to provide accurate information in this book, but it is possible that errors and omissions have been introduced. Please consider this in making any career plans or other important decisions. Trust your own judgment above all else and in all things.

Trademarks: All brand names and product names used in this book are trade names, service marks, trademarks, or registered trademarks of their respective owners.

ISBN 978-1-59357-664-6

FOREWORD

Ever since the first scientific paper on emotional intelligence was published in 1990 by Jack Mayer and Peter Salovey, there has been an explosion of research, publications, books, and articles on the subject. I don't think anyone could have imagined the wide range of applications that this new idea would stimulate. In fact, a Google search on emotional intelligence will now provide you with more than 3.5 million hits.

The practical application of emotional intelligence began largely in the workplace. Emotional intelligence has been found to be useful in selecting employees, developing people, and training leaders. Other applications have evolved in dealing with families, children, health issues, and social and academic success. One of the reasons emotional intelligence has sustained itself, where many other ideas have come and gone, has been because researchers have been able to successfully measure it. The ability to measure emotional intelligence, through instruments such as the EQ-i (Emotional Quotient Inventory) and the MSCEIT (Mayer-Salovey-Caruso Emotional Intelligence Test), has given the concept scientific rigor.

In this book, Lisa Caldas Kappesser presents another application of emotional intelligence. She details the importance of emotional intelligence for people starting or changing their jobs. This book is geared to people who want to improve their chances of getting the job that's right for them. By becoming more emotionally aware and learning to better manage your emotions, you increase the chances of not only aiming for the right job, but also presenting your best when trying to land that job.

Although there's no simple answer to getting the job of your dreams, especially during difficult economic times, the information and activities in this book may provide you with the extra edge you need to get that job you've always wanted. So read this book, use the activities and exercises, and get yourself ready for that next job interview. Just as you need that extra "edge" in getting noticed, most organizations today need and want people who can provide them with the extra edge it takes to be successful in today's economy.

Steven J. Stein, Ph.D.

CEO, Multi-Health Systems;
author of *Emotional Intelligence for Dummies;*
and coauthor of *The EQ Edge: Emotional
Intelligence and Your Success*

DEDICATION

This book is dedicated to my husband and soul mate, Randy, for his love and support in fulfilling my dreams; my two daughters, Kaitlyn and Christine, for enriching my life beyond what words can say; and my parents, Richard and Janet Caldas, for their constant love and inspiration.

CONTENTS

INTRODUCTION

I first learned about emotional intelligence in 2002 when I became a member of a Consultants Roundtable made of individuals from area mental health organizations. I then read Daniel Goleman's book *Emotional Intelligence: Why It Can Matter More than IQ,* and I became convinced how important this ability was in living healthy and productive lives. I saw it in my personal life and in my counseling work with children and families. I saw it in the administration of the organizations and at the schools where I worked. Since that time, I have continued to be an active learner of emotional intelligence, reading books, articles, and research, as well as developing programs for colleges and businesses and using it in my career coaching practice. In this book, I apply my knowledge and experience from my background in psychology, my 20+ years of counseling experience as a licensed social worker, my training to become a certified coach, my own personal and professional experiences in changing jobs and making a career transition, and my training and experience in working with individuals who are in career transition or who want to improve their emotional intelligence skills and performance in their career.

My goal in writing this book is to help job seekers understand emotional intelligence (or EQ for short) and apply it to the challenging task of finding, getting, and keeping a satisfying job. In the competitive job market, I believe that using your emotional intelligence can give you the edge and set you apart from the other job candidates. I also believe that having an underdeveloped emotional intelligence can hurt your job search performance and keep you from landing the job you want. Using your EQ is not only important in landing the job, but it also is helpful in selecting the right occupation and job and performing effectively in your new job or career.

Emotional Intelligence Basics

Your cognitive intelligence and your personality are two traits that theorists believe you are born with, and these traits do not change much. Your emotional intelligence, however, is believed to develop as you experience life and interact with others and your environment. Everyone has emotional intelligence to some degree or level.

In Part I of this book, I provide working models of emotional intelligence and of its building blocks, both of which I have developed and adapted from my training and experience. The building block model, the EQ Connection Triangle, shows how your thoughts, feelings, and behaviors are all connected and how they affect one another. By reflecting on this connection, you will develop and use emotional intelligence to achieve your desired outcome. Part I also includes a quiz that I developed that you can take to give you an idea of your level of emotional intelligence.

I break down emotional intelligence into four distinct skill sets:

- **Self-awareness:** This set includes the skills of emotion identification, accurate self-assessment, and self-confidence.

- **Self-management:** This set includes the skills of emotional self-control, adaptability, stress management, and motivation/optimism.

- **Social awareness:** This set includes the skills of empathy, reality testing, and social responsibility.

- **Social skills:** This set includes the skills of trust and honesty, communication and assertiveness, cooperation and collaboration, conflict management and negotiation, and influence on and development of others.

Part II describes each of these skills in detail and explains how you can apply them in job search situations. In addition, the EQ Exercise worksheets throughout this book will help you grow these skills. I also draw from my experiences as a career coach to tell you what happens when EQ skills are put to the test in the Emotional Intelligence in Action sidebars (all names and identifying information have been changed).

In Part III, I focus on how to show off your EQ to make the connection with the interviewer and further your advantage in getting the job offer. I will describe some of the typical job search obstacles that may interfere in your career transition, as well as provide strategies and exercises to overcome them. Lastly, I will share examples and exercises on how to continue using your EQ skills to achieve success in your new job.

Research evidence continues to grow that supports the usefulness of emotional intelligence in many diverse areas. I will not focus on research studies in this book, but instead impart the knowledge learned from the research findings as it relates to the areas of discussion. I include references in the back of this book for your further reading and research.

The Career Transition Process

Before you dig into the details of EQ and the job search, take a moment to consider the career transition process. Any job search or career transition entails stages or phases that you travel through to get from start to finish. This means that certain tasks are helpful if completed before other ones, and tasks often build upon one another. You can use the following list of stages of the career transition process as a map to guide you in your job search:

The Career Transition Process

I. Managing emotions/self-assessment

II. Exploring career options

III. Targeting specific jobs and careers

IV. Interviewing for positions

V. Negotiating and accepting a job offer

The greater your EQ, the greater your advantage in maneuvering through the job search process effectively and in landing the job. It is helpful to know what stage you are in at any point in time and to evaluate how you are using your EQ knowledge to reach your goals.

Each of the emotional intelligence skills is important in the career transition process to land the right job. However, in each stage, certain EQ skills are definitely needed or emphasized more to produce the desired outcome. As a general overview, here are the skills emphasized in each stage:

Stage of Career Transition	EQ Skill Emphasized
I. Managing emotions/self-assessment	Self-awareness
II. Exploring career options	Social awareness
III. Targeting specific jobs and careers	Self-awareness and social awareness
IV. Interviewing for positions	Self-management and social skills
V. Negotiating and accepting a job offer	Social skills

You can see how important it is to develop your self-awareness and your social awareness before you can fully use your self-management and social skills in reaching your goal of landing the right job and in maximizing the terms of your job offer. Can someone with low self-awareness be high in self-management? Yes. They may tolerate stress really well (self-management) but have difficulty identifying and expressing their feelings (self-awareness). Would having more self-awareness help that person manage himself even better? Yes. However, everyone has some level of each of these skills, and these skills work together. Whatever areas of EQ that are strengths for you mean that you will perform those particular career transition activities at a higher level. This is how using your EQ and making it stronger can give you the edge over other job seekers.

The table on the following page is an overview of how emotional intelligence is integrated in reaching your goals. Each area leads to development and achievement in the next area. In the chapters ahead, you will see how thought-feeling-behavior connections are the building blocks for emotional intelligence skills. As you identify your EQ skills, you can see which ones need to be used more at any point in the career transition process. By applying your skills throughout the job search, you are more likely to perform better, take the competitive advantage over others, and obtain the outcome that you want. I will give you information, examples, and exercises to develop your connections and thus your skills and then show you how you can use these skills in the career transition process to reach your goals and ultimately land the right job for you.

Building Blocks of EQ⟶	EQ Skills⟶	Career Transition Stage⟶	Career Goals
Thought-feeling-behavior connections	**Self-awareness** - emotion identification - accurate self-assessment - self-confidence	I. Managing emotions/self-assessment	Find the right career
		II. Exploring career options	Select the right job in that career
	Self-management - self-control - adaptability - stress management - motivation/optimism	III. Targeting specific jobs and careers	Get the job offer
		IV. Interviewing for positions	Be successful in your chosen career
	Social awareness - empathy - reality testing - social responsibility	V. Negotiating and accepting a job offer	
	Social skills - trust and honesty - communication/assertiveness - cooperation/collaboration - conflict management/negotiation - influencing and developing others		

ACKNOWLEDGMENTS

First and foremost I thank God, for He has blessed me with many gifts and in Him all things are possible. I thank my husband and daughters, who have been so patient with me through this whole book-writing process as it has taken much of my time and energies. I thank my parents, who taught me to strive to be the best I can be and instilled in me the belief that I could do anything I wanted to. I am thankful for my sisters for encouraging me along the way but for also keeping me humble, and to the Kappesser family whom I am lucky to be a part of and whom I admire for their sense of love, loyalty, and commitment to each other. Life would not be as rich, of course, if it were not for all my good friends and book club companions who have shared my excitement and supported my endeavors.

I would like to thank Associate Publisher Sue Pines, who took a chance on me in publishing this book, and I thank her for her gentle guidance in walking me through this venture. I thank my editor, Heather Stith, who used her expertise to make this book interesting and to make the content flow so easily for the reader.

I admire and appreciate the influence and contributions of all the leaders in the field of emotional intelligence. I give special mention to Steven Stein, Daniel Goleman, Peter Salovey, John Mayer, Reuven Bar-On, Adele Lynn, Relly Nadler, and the Consortium for Research on Emotional Intelligence in Organizations who have shaped my work in emotional intelligence.

I want to acknowledge the works and influence of Albert Ellis, Aaron Beck, Martin Seligman, Howard Gardner, and other great leaders in the field of psychology who have shaped my knowledge and work in counseling and coaching.

I would like to acknowledge the training and support from my mentor coaches, beginning with Jeff Auerbach, president and coaching leader of the College of Executive Coaching where I received my coach training/certification; Lewis Lubin, who expanded my business expertise; and Vicki Wolfe, Barbara Czestochowa, Gregg Oshita, and Michael Lynch, all coaches whom I emulate. I also am thankful to my educators in the field of career development and transition.

A special thanks to my counseling mentors and supervisors, who taught me how to use my talent and training to help others lead higher quality lives, with special mention to Cathy Douglas-Penn for providing me the opportunity to begin this adventure by participating in a Consultants Roundtable on emotional intelligence; Kristina Chesson for having the confidence in me to develop and implement an emotional intelligence program in her school, from where my passion for emotional intelligence began; and JoAnn Payne and Michele Schuster for their support and promotion of my coaching business.

Last and most importantly, I want to thank all of my counseling and coaching clients for allowing me to partner with them in reaching their personal and professional goals.

For More Personal Help with Your Career

My passion is in helping others succeed. I can assist you in person, by phone, or online with assessments and career coaching in any of the following areas:

- Online assessments: EQ-i, Myers-Briggs Type Indicator, and Strong Interest Inventory
- Career coaching: Career exploration, resume development, networking, and interviewing
- Coaching for Strategic Career Advancement
- Coaching for Leadership Development
- Emotional Intelligence Skill Training and Coaching

I also enjoy speaking to groups and organizations about emotional intelligence and career-related topics. If interested, please contact me:

Lisa Caldas Kappesser, MA
President
EQ Coaching Solutions, LLC
Web site: www.eqcoachingsolutions.com
E-mail: info@eqcoachingsolutions.com
Phone: 1-513-312-7856

PART I

Understanding Emotional Intelligence and Discovering Your EQ

Part I defines emotional intelligence in a way that you can understand and use:

- Chapter 1, "Emotional Intelligence: Understand Your Job Search Advantage," teaches you the importance of EQ in being successful in reaching your goals, with particular focus on the job search process. The exercises in this chapter help you to identify emotional intelligence qualities in the people you interact with at work and in your personal life. This chapter wraps up with a quiz that you can take to assess your emotional intelligence.

- Chapter 2, "EQ Building Blocks: Connect Your Thoughts, Feelings, and Behaviors," explains how understanding and using the connections between your thoughts, emotions, and behaviors can increase your EQ. This chapter provides an overview of the biological and psychological basis for emotional intelligence. This chapter also describes some techniques to use in order to change your thoughts and steer yourself toward your goals.

Emotional Intelligence: Understand Your Job Search Advantage

In this chapter, I explain what emotional intelligence is and tell you why it is important to you. As I explain what emotional intelligence is all about, you will likely think it is common sense. You may take your emotional intelligence for granted, or you may not understand the impact that it has and how it can make a difference in your performance. But your emotional intelligence can give you an advantage in the job market today, because many employers are looking for people with high emotional intelligence. Employers have even developed structured interview questions that tap into emotional intelligence, because research has convinced them that such intelligence is a critical part of developing high potentials, star performers, and leaders.

The good news is that, unlike your IQ (Intellectual Quotient), your emotional intelligence can be improved and developed. The first step is to read this chapter and take the emotional intelligence quiz at the end to identify areas of strength and weakness in your emotional intelligence. With the help of the exercises throughout this book, you will learn how to develop and apply your emotional intelligence to choose the best career for you, target the right position, get the job offer, and succeed at work.

What Is Emotional Intelligence?

The definition of emotional intelligence varies. The term *emotional intelligence* was conceived by Drs. Peter Salovey and John Mayer in 1990. In the book *Emotional Development and Emotional Intelligence: Educational Implications,* they describe it as *"the ability to perceive emotions, to access and generate emotions so as to assist thought, to understand emotions and emotional meanings, and to reflectively regulate emotions so as to promote both better emotion and thought."*

Daniel Goleman, inspired by Salovey and Mayer's work, popularized the concept with the release of his book *Emotional Intelligence: Why It Can Matter More Than IQ* in 1995. Goleman's definition of emotional intelligence, as stated in his book *Working with Emotional Intelligence,* is the

"capacity for recognizing our own feelings and those of others, for motivating ourselves, and for managing emotions well in ourselves and our relationships."

Reuven Bar-On developed the term *EQ,* which stands for Emotional Quotient, and created the EQ-i assessment to measure emotional intelligence. In the technical manual *EQ-i Bar-On Emotional Quotient Inventory: A Measure of Emotional Intelligence,* he defines emotional intelligence as

"an array of non-cognitive capabilities, competencies, and skills that influence one's ability to succeed in coping with environmental demands and pressures."

My working definition or model of emotional intelligence focuses mainly on Daniel Goleman's discussion of personal and social competencies and Reuven Bar-On's model of emotional intelligence, in which he points out how these competencies impact mood and effective performance. The skills that I describe in the chapters ahead are a combination of the skills and competencies that these authors use to represent emotional intelligence in their emotional intelligence assessments.

To make the concept of emotional intelligence more understandable and usable, I have simplified the definition. Emotional intelligence is a group of four skill sets or competencies that, when used together effectively, can help you achieve your desired impact or outcome. To remember what these skill sets are, think of 4S:

- Self-awareness

- Self-management

- Social awareness

- Social skills

Part II of this book explains each of these skill sets in detail and describes how to use them in every aspect of your job search.

Why Is Emotional Intelligence Important?

When utilized effectively, emotional intelligence can help you reach your goals. Figure 1.1 shows how all the different emotional intelligence skill sets fit together in this process. By using and combining your personal and social competencies, you can achieve your desired outcome.

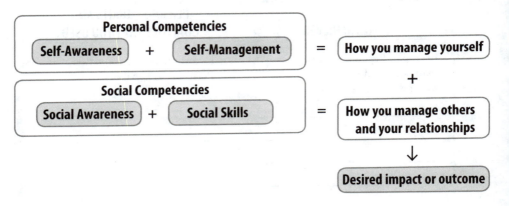

Figure 1.1. The emotional intelligence process.

The following sections highlight the research that explains how emotional intelligence factors in achievement.

Emotional Intelligence Is Linked with Success

Success is achieving or accomplishing your goals, whatever those goals are for you. Research such as that from the Consortium for Research on Emotional Intelligence in Organizations (which you can visit at www.eiconsortium.org) demonstrates how emotional intelligence skills are instrumental in achieving success and business results. When you reflect on what has enabled you to achieve success in your life, it likely involves emotional intelligence qualities.

EQ EXERCISE: REFLECT ON WHAT HAS MADE YOU SUCCESSFUL

You have goals in many different areas of your life, such as the goal to lose weight or complete a certification program. In this exercise, write down some of the goals that you have achieved. List the traits or qualities that you think helped you to reach those goals. Include goals in all areas of your life, such as career, family, education, and health.

GOALS ACHIEVED	PERSONAL TRAITS AND QUALITIES THAT YOU USED
Example: Began and maintained an exercise routine of 3 days a week.	Determination, Motivation, Persistence, Flexibility, Optimism, Organization

Look at the qualities you listed and compare them with the following list of emotional intelligence skills, gathered from the many authors I mentioned earlier. Do any of these skills appear in your answers? Circle the qualities that you listed that are related to emotional intelligence. You may want to repeat this exercise after reading the next few chapters in which I explain all of the following emotional intelligence traits in greater detail and give you examples for each of them.

Emotional Intelligence Skills

Being aware of your emotions	Being socially responsible
Having self-confidence	Controlling your emotions
Managing stress	Adapting to change
Staying motivated and optimistic	Showing empathy
Having a good sense of reality	Knowing your strengths and weaknesses
Trusting others and being honest	Communicating well and being assertive
Cooperating and collaborating with others	Managing conflict and negotiating
Having strong relationships with others	Having influence and being persuasive

Emotional Intelligence Helps You Make the Most of Your Other Qualities

Your physical features and personal qualities are what they are. Your IQ is fixed. The amount of education and experience that you currently have is a given. Using your emotional intelligence can give you the edge in maximizing what you have in the way of appearance, IQ, education, and work experiences by reflecting on, identifying, and shaping any of these areas to bring about a positive impact or outcome.

EMOTIONAL INTELLIGENCE IN ACTION

If you use your emotional intelligence to reflect on how you look and how you are perceived by others, you can then make small changes that may have big effects. Harry is in project management with more than 20 years of experience in engineering and information technology. He is in his late 40s and wants to pursue a position as a CEO for a nationwide rifle organization. Based on his years of volunteer work in setting up competitions and promoting this sport, he seems to be well qualified. After several meetings with his career coach, he makes some significant changes to his appearance. He wears a blazer and nice pair of pants instead of jeans to the next meeting. He sports a new, shorter hair-style that makes him look more youthful. Instead of contacts, he wears glasses, which make him look more intellectual. When he asks his career coach for feed-back about the changes in his appearance, she says that she thinks that they are all positive changes. He now looks like a CEO.

Being good-looking and being smart in general are traits that attract and can help you to connect with others, including potential employers. These qualities generally do not hurt or work against you, and they can be advantages if you use them in the right way. The fact is that you will be competing for jobs with people who are more attractive than you, as well as those who are less attractive. You also will be competing for jobs with people both smarter and dumber than you. It makes sense to use what you have to the fullest.

In the book *Emotional Intelligence: Why It Can Matter More Than IQ,* author Daniel Goleman makes the point that EQ is just as important if not more important than IQ. I believe you can use your EQ to make the most of your IQ. For example, emotional intelligence can help you use your cognitive intelligence to achieve your educational goals. Yes, you need to have a certain amount of cognitive intelligence or IQ to handle certain courses, but studies have shown that success also comes from self-discipline, motivation, and adaptability, which are all emotional intelligence skills. You can be successful in completing a course only if you are motivated and disciplined enough to do the work as well as able to adapt to changes in your life or overcome obstacles that get in the way.

EMOTIONAL INTELLIGENCE IN ACTION

Nasir is a chemical engineer for a top consumer goods company. He is very smart, and he knows it. He acts with high confidence and tends to be critical of others when they challenge his ideas. He always acts like the smartest guy in the room. So how do his peers view him and work with him? They admit he is smart, but they also say he is very difficult to work with, unyielding, opinionated, and rude. His fellow team members do not feel that he values their ideas and input, so they do not view him as a team player. Nasir is cognitively smart and does his job well when it comes to independent work. However, he is not fully successful or productive in his job because he is lacking interpersonal skills.

Nasir is not likely to be a good manager, either, because of his abrasiveness and know-it-all attitude. His potential subordinates would likely not be open with him due to fear of repercussion or because they do not like him. They may feel instead a need to put up barriers to protect themselves from his criticisms to save their job positions. In the end, Nasir will not progress to a management position—even though he is smart enough cognitively to take on such a position—because he does not have the social skills. He would be more effective if he used his personal and social skills in a way to leverage his other strengths.

You can use your emotional intelligence to outweigh any limitations that you feel you have in regards to education or experience. Using your emotional intelligence skills of self-awareness and social awareness, you might decide to make changes in the areas of education or experience. You might go back to college to obtain more education or increase your experience in a given area by seeking out that kind of work, even if it means you have to volunteer or give away your services.

Emotional Intelligence Helps You Connect with Others

You can interact with and affect others in both positive and negative ways. Yet you are more likely to reach your desired outcome or goals by interacting positively and connecting with others.

I use the word *likeable* to describe people with high emotional intelligence, because they are people whom you like being around. Why? Likeable people give off positive energy, and you pick up on their energy. It affects you in a positive way, and you feel good.

EQ EXERCISE: DESCRIBE WHAT MAKES SOMEONE LIKEABLE

Think of family members, coworkers, and other people whom you enjoy being with. In the space provided, list their names and their likeable traits.

LIKEABLE PEOPLE	QUALITIES THAT MAKE THEM LIKEABLE
_____	_____
_____	_____
_____	_____
_____	_____
_____	_____
_____	_____
_____	_____
_____	_____

Look at the traits that you listed and circle those that are emotional intelligence traits by looking at the previous Emotional Intelligence Skills list. My guess is that you have listed many emotional intelligence traits to describe these people.

Likeable people are usually people who are in touch with how they feel, manage their emotions and behaviors well, and seem to be in tune with others and the situation at hand. Likeable people engage others easily, display a sense of humor, are outwardly optimistic, and don't get too anxious or bogged down with stress. In the same way you like to be around these kinds of people, potential employers also like them and want to add them to their organizations.

One of the school principals I worked with exemplified emotional intelligence. She acted with honesty and integrity and followed through on her commitments to others. She made time for everyone and communicated very openly and confidently with students, teachers, parents, other administrators, volunteers, and community officials. She was emotionally sensitive but strong and seemed to know what to say and how to respond in various situations. She was slow to anger and patient and rarely seemed stressed or overwhelmed. She showed genuine interest and concern in people by the questions she asked. She was goal oriented, motivated, and committed. She was realistic but positive and displayed a gentle sense of humor. Her ability to connect with others helped her to raise the school's proficiency rating, which takes joint effort from students, parents, and teachers.

In contrast, one of the teachers I worked with was definitely lacking in EQ (and was not likeable, in my view). She always came to school in a negative mood and would openly share her frustration. And she seemed to have a new frustration every day! She would draw upon the school politics and talk about the senselessness of it all, as if nothing she did really mattered. She was very self-centered and rarely asked how I was doing or what I thought about the topic at hand. I began to avoid her as much as possible. She felt too heavy, and I felt overwhelmed. I even felt a twinge of hopelessness as I left her room. Her negative emotions were contagious, but I don't think she really knew or understood the impact she had on others. If she affected me in this way, how was she affecting others, especially her students and other teachers on her team?

EQ EXERCISE: DESCRIBE WHAT MAKES SOMEONE NOT LIKEABLE

Think of people whom you do not like to be around. (I am sure you can come up with a few.) How do you feel when you are with them? What pushes you away or turns you off? What makes them less likeable than others? List these people and the qualities that make them not likeable.

NOT LIKEABLE PEOPLE	QUALITIES THAT MAKE THEM NOT LIKEABLE

(continued)

(continued)

NOT LIKEABLE PEOPLE	QUALITIES THAT MAKE THEM NOT LIKEABLE
_____	_____
_____	_____
_____	_____
_____	_____
_____	_____
_____	_____
_____	_____
_____	_____
_____	_____
_____	_____

Look at the qualities that you listed. They are likely the opposite of the emotional intelligence skills listed earlier. These people are likely lower in emotional intelligence, or they are not using their skills.

Being emotionally intelligent can make you more likeable and thus enable you to connect with others. Being likeable in and of itself will not get you the job, but it is an asset in the job search process.

Emotional Intelligence Skills Can Be Improved at Any Age

Studies support the idea that, unlike IQ, emotional intelligence or EQ can be developed and improved at any age. Psychological assessment publisher Multi-Health Systems, Inc., facilitated a study of almost 4,000 people in Canada and the United States that concluded that EQ rises steadily from the late teen years until the 40s and then tapers off during the 50s for both men and women. (Authors Steven Stein and Howard Book mention this study in their book, *The EQ Edge: Emotional Intelligence and Your Success*.) It makes sense that these kinds of skills would grow with age, experience, and wisdom from life's lessons.

I am one of many who advocate teaching young children emotional intelligence skills. If schools would focus on developing their students' emotional and social competencies, they would improve students' ability to use their cognitive and academic skills, which would in turn improve learning and thus increase proficiency scores, which is the goal by which schools are measured. I implemented an emotional intelligence training program in a fourth grade classroom with support from the principal and teachers. After completing the program, the students showed an increase of 30 percent in their emotional intelligence skills. Office referrals to the principal for student misconduct were reduced by 50 percent from the first quarter to the fourth quarter. The teachers reported that the classroom became a better learning environment because students got along better and there were fewer distractions. These students took their improved skills into future classrooms and into their daily interactions.

Employers Are Looking for Emotional Intelligence

Organizations are learning the importance of EQ and understanding how emotionally intelligent employees lead to the development of better teams, higher performance and productivity, and thus results. Managers are using structured interview questions to tap into an applicant's personal and social competencies. Some organizations even use emotional intelligence assessments as part of the selection process.

Your goal in the job interview is to make a connection with the interviewer. If you are likeable, you are starting off on the right foot. Sharper EQ awareness and communication of your traits and their importance to the bottom line of the business will sell your value and benefit to the employer and will make you a desirable candidate. Emotional intelligence skills are important in the job search and can give you an advantage over others who do not use these skills to the fullest.

Once you land a job, having a high EQ is sure to give you an edge in your job performance. For example, stress management is an emotional intelligence skill and is necessary for effective performance. EQ is about managing yourself and others effectively to bring about satisfactory results for you, your coworkers, your customers, and your employer.

EQ Can Help with Career Choice and Targeting the Right Job

Of course, some occupations seem to require more emotional intelligence than others. Knowing which EQ skills are required to do well in an occupation and determining whether you have them can help you in selecting the right occupation for you. Emphasizing your strengths in these required EQ skills can also help you get hired.

For example, teachers and salespeople need empathy. The EQ skill of empathy is about being able to see things from another's perspective. In teaching and selling, it is crucial for teachers to understand their students and for salespeople to know their customers. If teachers cannot read the students that they are teaching and understand what they are feeling and thinking, they will not connect with them and will not be able to successfully teach them. For example, take a student who is unable to learn because of a dysfunctional family life in which there is constant stress. If the teacher ignores the student's condition and does not get some professional help for him, the teacher's educational efforts will be unproductive. The student cannot be receptive and assimilate the information in his current state of functioning. He is overwhelmed with emotions and related thoughts of what is going on at home. Emotionally intelligent teachers understand this. They value the student and the student's work, and they advocate for the student and get and give the help and support the student needs in order to learn.

Salespeople demonstrate empathy by showing respect and understanding of customers' needs as well as a desire to assist the customers. Sales is about building honest, trusting relationships with customers. First, salespeople try to connect with customers by being likeable and maybe displaying a sense of humor. Then salespeople build on those connections to influence customers to ultimately buy products. Think back to times you had to buy an appliance, and there were salespeople whom you liked and those whom you did not like. If the products were comparable in quality and price, you probably bought from the salesperson whom you liked and trusted.

Emotional Intelligence Is Critical to Effective Leadership

Daniel Goleman wrote the article "What Makes a Good Leader?" which appeared in the *Harvard Business Review* in 1998 and continues to be one of its most requested articles. In this article, he highlighted the importance of emotional intelligence skills for managers. Being and acting with emotional intelligence can be critical to developing others, motivating teams, reaching organizational goals, and bringing about business results. People can understand and see the power of emotional intelligence everyday in their interactions and relationships with their bosses.

EQ EXERCISE: IDENTIFY WHAT MAKES A BOSS LIKEABLE

Just as you looked at likeable acquaintances, you can look back to bosses whom you liked. Write down adjectives in the second column to describe the bosses that you list in the first column.

LIKEABLE BOSSES	QUALITIES THAT MAKE THEM LIKEABLE

(continued)

(continued)

How many of the qualities that you listed are emotional intelligence traits? Go back and circle them. You have likely circled many EQ skills.

Did these bosses do or say things that showed that they valued you and/or your work? How did you feel when they showed their appreciation for you and for your work? Did this in turn affect your work performance and attitude? When you feel you and your work are valued, you feel productive and that you are making a contribution or a difference. These good feelings energize you and motivate you to continue working and achieving your goals.

It has been said that people more often leave bosses than they leave the actual jobs. People may like the career or the job position, but they are unable to function well with their boss and thus try to find another job in the same company or leave the organization altogether. Emotionally intelligent managers are critical in retaining and motivating employees and are therefore important to an organization's ongoing success. Emotional intelligence skills are seen as so important that some companies are even investing in personal coaching for their employees—especially for high potentials, as well as for current and future leaders—so that they can develop these skills.

EQ EXERCISE: IDENTIFY WHAT MAKES A BOSS NOT LIKEABLE

List bosses whom you did not like and list what they did or said that made them not likeable.

NOT LIKEABLE BOSSES	QUALITIES THAT MAKE THEM NOT LIKEABLE

NOT LIKEABLE BOSSES	QUALITIES THAT MAKE THEM NOT LIKEABLE
_____	_____
_____	_____
_____	_____
_____	_____
_____	_____
_____	_____
_____	_____
_____	_____
_____	_____

How many of these listed bosses have high levels of emotional intelligence? Likely very few. These bosses probably treated you and/or your work as less than valuable. How did you feel in these situations, and how did it affect your work? Feeling angry is normal. Hurt feelings often accompany the anger because such treatment can be a blow to your ego and can make you feel disrespected. When you feel this way, you certainly are not going to respond positively or feel motivated. You might respond by not doing your work or by doing only the bare minimum. Thus this loss of meaning and motivation makes you become less productive.

What Is Your EQ?

Just as you have an IQ that can be measured by an IQ test, your EQ can be obtained through an EQ assessment. Although getting an accurate assessment of your EQ score requires a more rigorous test, the quiz in this section can give you a rough idea about your EQ strengths and weaknesses. Most importantly, it will indicate what areas you can improve to be more effective in landing the right job for you.

For a more in-depth picture of your EQ, consider taking the EQ-i assessment. Reuven Bar-On developed this assessment to answer the question, "Why do some people with high IQs fail in life while others succeed?"

One's EQ seemed to make a difference and was not highly correlated with IQ. The EQ-i was the first validated instrument across culture and gender with high reliability and validity. (This work was accomplished with the help of Dr. Steven Stein and Multi-Health Systems, Inc. [MHS for short].)

You can take the EQ-i and obtain your EQ score online through a career coach who is trained and certified in administering and interpreting the assessment. In general, working with a coach is a great way to develop your emotional intelligence skills. Meeting regularly with your coach over a period of time allows you time to practice and then time to evaluate your progress with an objective person. (See the section "For More Personal Help with Your Career" in the introduction to this book for more information.)

EXERCISE: ASSESS YOUR EQ

In order to rate your emotional intelligence skills as you approach your job search, assess how these statements pertain to you.

STATEMENT	SELDOM	SOMETIMES	OFTEN	USUALLY
1. I am aware of my feelings at any given moment.	❏	❏	❏	❏
2. I am aware of my daily moods.	❏	❏	❏	❏
3. I know what triggers my anger and frustration in my job search.	❏	❏	❏	❏
4. I know what strengths I can offer to employers.	❏	❏	❏	❏
5. I know my weaknesses and how they impact my actions.	❏	❏	❏	❏
6. I am confident that I have much to offer a new employer.	❏	❏	❏	❏
7. I manage my anger without much difficulty.	❏	❏	❏	❏
8. I am patient with myself and with others as I search for my next job.	❏	❏	❏	❏

STATEMENT	SELDOM	SOMETIMES	OFTEN	USUALLY
9. I manage stress without becoming too frazzled.	❒	❒	❒	❒
10. I can deal easily with change.	❒	❒	❒	❒
11. I am comfortable in trying new things.	❒	❒	❒	❒
12. I see obstacles as a challenge and strive to find solutions.	❒	❒	❒	❒
13. I am self-motivated and do not need external rewards or incentives.	❒	❒	❒	❒
14. My past coworkers would say I understand and support them.	❒	❒	❒	❒
15. I am able to read others fairly well by what they do and say.	❒	❒	❒	❒
16. My past coworkers would say I have a good handle on seeing things as they truly are.	❒	❒	❒	❒
17. I am good at assessing the reality of a situation and try to face it openly.	❒	❒	❒	❒
18. I like to help others and serve the community that I am a part of.	❒	❒	❒	❒
19. My past coworkers would say I am often thinking of others and the group as a whole.	❒	❒	❒	❒
20. My past coworkers would describe me as an honest person.	❒	❒	❒	❒
21. I communicate openly and will express my views without offending others.	❒	❒	❒	❒

(continued)

(continued)

STATEMENT	SELDOM	SOMETIMES	OFTEN	USUALLY
22. My past coworkers would describe me as a good team player.	❒	❒	❒	❒
23. I am able to maintain my work and personal relationships and develop new ones.	❒	❒	❒	❒
24. I deal with disagreements openly and with confidence.	❒	❒	❒	❒
25. Others would say that I inspire and encourage them to reach their goals.	❒	❒	❒	❒
26. Others would say that I value and respect them and the work that they do.	❒	❒	❒	❒

Scoring

Total the number of checks in each column: ＿＿＿＿ ＿＿＿＿ ＿＿＿＿ ＿＿＿＿

Multiply this number by: ×1 ×2 ×3 ×4

Add these four numbers: ＿＿＿＿ ＿＿＿＿ ＿＿＿＿ ＿＿＿＿

Total:＿＿＿＿＿

What Your Score Means

A score of 78 or more shows you are using your emotional intelligence to your advantage. Read through the chapters and exercises ahead for a better assessment, and talk to your family, friends, or a mentor to get more feedback.

A score of 52–77 shows some emotional intelligence strengths but also some underused skills that if improved will help you to reach your goals. Read through the chapters and exercises ahead for a better assessment of strengths and weaknesses.

A score of 51 or below shows unused emotional intelligence skills and opportunities for growth. This book can help you identify ways to develop your skills to be more successful in your job search and career.

Now go back and draw a line under statements 6, 13, and 19. You now have 4 groupings of statements. Count the number of check marks that you have in the Often and Usually columns for each grouping and write the number on the line below. Compare your numbers. The highest number shows an area of strength for you. The lowest number represents an area of EQ that is the weakest.

Statements 1–6: Self-awareness   _____

Statements 7–13: Self-management   _____

Statements 14–19: Social awareness   _____

Statements 20–26: Social skills   _____

It is more important to focus on which area you can grow rather than your total score. By working on a particular skill area, you can be more focused in your development and evaluate your progress more clearly over time.

Now that you know which emotional intelligence skills you have to improve, how do you go about developing these skills, and how do you gauge your improvement? In the pages ahead, I explain these skills in great detail and give you exercises that help you develop your EQ skills. I provide strategies and tips on how to use your EQ through the career transition process and into your new job. You will know you are successful in raising your EQ when you accomplish your goals and reflect on the particular EQ skills that you used to help you. You can use the exercises that follow to help yourself and to monitor your progress, but keep in mind that you will only be as effective as you are honest with yourself.

Chapter Reflections

Emotional intelligence is about identifying and managing your emotions, thoughts, and behaviors, while taking into account others' emotions, thoughts, and behaviors and acting in a way that moves you toward your desired outcome or goal. Most people are aware of their feelings and how those feelings drive their actions, but fewer people can identify how their feelings affect their performance and their relationships.

I define emotional intelligence as the four skill sets of self-awareness, self-management, social awareness, and social skills that, when used together effectively, can help you achieve your desired impact or outcome. These skills are important for several reasons:

- Emotional intelligence is linked with success. When you reflect on what has enabled you to achieve success in your life, it likely involves emotional intelligence skills.

- Emotional intelligence helps you make the most of your IQ, experience, education, and personal qualities such as physical appearance. Using your emotional intelligence is a process of reflecting on, identifying, and shaping any of these areas to bring about a more positive impact or outcome.

- Emotional intelligence helps you reach your goals by connecting with others. One way to describe emotionally intelligent people is likeable. Likeable people give off positive energy that spreads and affects others in positive ways and leaves a positive impact.

- You can increase your emotional intelligence at any age.

- Employers look for emotional intelligence when they hire. EQ can give you an advantage in interviews and during your job search. EQ skills can help you with career choice and targeting the right job, as well as bring continued success in your new job or career. Research also supports the importance of emotional intelligence in determining effective leaders.

Now that you have a general idea of what emotional intelligence is, why it is important, and what your EQ might be, the next chapter explains how you can start to develop your EQ to help your job search and career.

EQ Building Blocks: Connect Your Thoughts, Feelings, and Behaviors

In the last chapter, you learned that your EQ is not a static number. You can change it. But exactly how does this change occur? It starts in the brain. By reflecting on the connections between your thoughts, feelings, and behaviors, you grow your neural circuitry. You can then change your thoughts and behaviors in service of your goals and desired outcomes. In this chapter, you will learn how to challenge your thoughts or try on behaviors to affect change in your emotions and in your ongoing actions.

Understanding the Biological Basis of Emotional Intelligence

In the book *Emotional Intelligence: Why It Can Matter More Than IQ*, author Daniel Goleman explores the idea that developing your emotional intelligence creates physical changes in your brain. He shares research in the field of neuroscience that shows how the connections between neurons develop to connect thought and emotion centers in the brain. Individuals who develop strong pathways between these centers develop higher emotional intelligence.

To understand how this process works, you need a general understanding of brain anatomy (see Figure 2.1). Stimuli enter the brain through the brain stem, which is in the back of the brain. Stimuli progress to the limbic system, located in the center of the brain, which is where emotions are processed and experienced. You then experience an emotional reaction without any rational thought connected to it. The rational part of the brain, where data analysis and decision making occurs, is located in the neocortex in the outer part of the brain. So in order to connect emotions to thoughts and derive a decision on how to respond, the limbic system and the neocortex need to work together. The more they work together, the more established the pathways between them become and thus the more developed your emotional intelligence becomes.

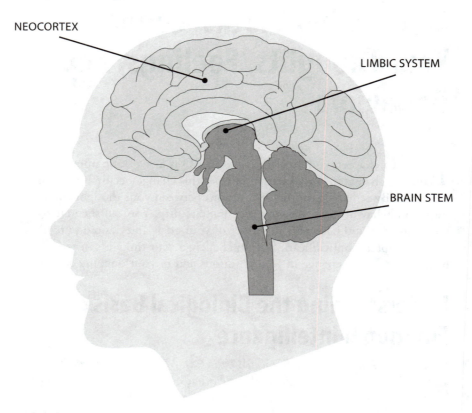

NEOCORTEX

LIMBIC SYSTEM

BRAIN STEM

Figure 2.1. Major parts of the brain.

How Emotional Intelligence Develops

Cognitive intelligence is developed when you add information and understanding to your memory banks in the neocortex. You take new data and new understandings and fit them into existing frameworks of association and understanding and thus extend and develop your neural circuitry. Cognitive intelligence can be developed through a traditional classroom approach in which the teacher lectures and students assimilate the information.

When you develop emotional intelligence, you incorporate data and make connections between two different areas of your brain: the neocortex and the limbic system. The best way to develop emotional intelligence is through an experiential learning approach in which the learner is more active in the learning process. The task becomes to weaken existing habits and patterns first and then create new ones. Through everyday trial-and-error behaviors and learning from mistakes, you incorporate new data and learning into existing circuitry, thus extending and strengthening neural pathways. Both cognitive and emotional intelligence develop as you interact in the environment.

One example of experiential learning is interactive workshops that involve some assessment of current skills, an understanding of what the desired behaviors look like, and exercises and practice of the new skills in and out of the workshop. Coaching is another example of experiential learning. During this process, coaches and their clients explore ideas, emotions, and behaviors in specific contexts. Clients take on the challenge of trying out new learning and skills in real work and life settings and come back to discuss progress or lack thereof with their coaches on a regular basis. In this way, clients connect their emotions, thoughts, and behaviors.

How Social Intelligence Develops

The social competencies of emotional intelligence—social awareness and social skills—are developed explicitly through interactions with others. Daniel Goleman, in his book *Social Intelligence*, shares research that supports and explains this idea in great detail. He states that you develop social intelligence (or social competencies) through incorporating new data derived from your social interactions into your existing understanding and competencies, thus developing new or enhanced levels of these skills.

Emotionally intelligent teachers can enhance the emotional and social functioning of their students simply through their teaching style and their daily interactions with students. Likewise, parents can improve their children's emotional and social functioning by interacting with them in an emotionally and socially intelligent way. Children learn from what their parents do as much as or more than from what they say.

I experienced this concept in action every day in my work as a child and family therapist. Some parents would come into my office with the idea that I was going to instantly fix their child's behavior problems. My first responsibility as a therapist was to help the parents understand that what they said and did created the opportunity for the child to change his or her responding behavior. I gave parents the education to help them help their child to change and develop effective behaviors.

Your current levels of emotional and social intelligence determine how you are able to understand and use the data you take in from the outside world. The more you develop the neural connections in your brain, the quicker you can process the information. At first, you will have to work at understanding and using the connections; it becomes easier the more you do it.

Experts in any field can look at data related to their field or situation quickly and make a good decision. For example, an experienced engineer can look at a blueprint and decide what needs to be changed. An experienced art historian can look at a work of art and determine whether it is an original work or a reproduction. The neural pathways in these experts are highly developed and often used. These pathways work efficiently because the experts have made connections between thoughts or ideas and emotions and behaviors related to their work over and over again.

Emotional and social intelligence work in the same way. The more emotionally and socially intelligent you become, the smarter and more effective you become in working and getting along with others. Having more-developed emotional and social intelligence also helps you use your cognitive intelligence to its full capacity because these different types of intelligence all interact. By developing your emotional and social intelligence, you are making the most of what you have.

Linking Your Thoughts, Feelings, and Behaviors

English philosopher Francis Bacon said, "Knowledge is power." Self-knowledge will yield you great personal power. You cannot change yourself if you are not aware of what needs to be changed and why it needs to be changed. Without good self-awareness, you cannot manage yourself effectively. If you cannot manage yourself well, it is difficult to manage others' emotions and behaviors. Emotional intelligence starts with self-awareness. Self-awareness is a process of becoming aware of your thoughts, feelings, and behaviors by reflecting on them, thinking about them, and then acknowledging your understanding of how they are connected. It is a kind of intrapersonal communication in which you are actively involved in the processing of internal messages. You send and receive your own messages about yourself and provide feedback to yourself in an ongoing internal process.

The Psychology of Self-Awareness

Where does this idea of internal communication come from? It has been described in the literature on cognitive therapy, which had its beginnings in 1960 with the publication of *The Self-Concept in Depression* by Aaron Beck and D. Stein and the 1962 publication of Albert Ellis's book *Reason and Emotion in Psychotherapy.* Known as the father of Rational Emotive Therapy, Albert Ellis developed the idea that you can keep your emotions from overwhelming you by reflecting on your thoughts, challenging them, and thus changing them.

In 1983, Howard Gardner published *Frames of Mind: The Theory of Multiple Intelligences.* He was one of the first to make the distinction between cognitive and emotional intelligence. He also discussed intrapersonal intelligence, which is the ability to look within oneself and be able to reflect on your own thought-feeling-behavior connections in any given moment and over time. Together, Ellis's and Gardner's works underpin the concept of emotional intelligence.

A Model for Increasing Your EQ

To help people understand the connection between thoughts, feelings, and behaviors, I have developed and used a working model I call the EQ Connection Triangle (see Figure 2.2). Once you understand how this model works, you can use it to improve your understanding and development of these connections and thus change the brain connections between the emotional and rational centers in your brain and increase your emotional intelligence.

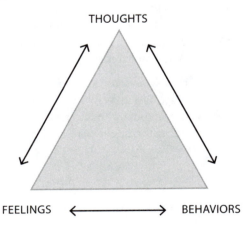

Figure 2.2. The EQ Connection Triangle.

Becoming self-aware and identifying the connections between your thoughts, feelings, and behaviors is the first step in increasing your emotional intelligence. The next step is to consciously choose to change one of the three areas (thoughts, feelings, or behaviors) with the goal of creating a certain outcome, making a certain impact, or attaining a particular goal. Changing one area will affect the other two areas.

The Roles of Feelings, Thoughts, and Behaviors in EQ

The basis of emotional intelligence is managing your emotions. You manage your emotions by reflecting on the related thoughts and behaviors that are creating them.

All emotions are meant to signal to you that an event is occurring outside of yourself and requires a response from you. Emotions are physiological signs and bodily cues that we label with feeling words. They are automatic self-protective mechanisms that have at their root the impulse to act.

Emotions also are objective, meaning they are what they are, they exist. They are not good or bad; they are neutral. However, you may place a value judgment on them. You may think happiness is a good emotion because it makes you feel euphoric or relaxed. You may label frustration as a bad emotion because it makes you feel anxious and uncomfortable. Changing or challenging a thought or behavior leads to a change in emotion. You cannot affect an emotion without first changing the thought and/ or behavior associated with it.

Thoughts are ideas or statements that you tell yourself. Your thoughts are driven by your needs, values, and beliefs, and you can challenge any of these and change them. Thoughts are *subjective* evaluations because they are open for questioning. You can explore their truth or reality.

Your behaviors are the actions you take in response to your feelings and thoughts. You can either react or act. When you *react,* you are just using your emotions. When you *act,* you are reflecting on both your emotions and the thoughts connected to them, evaluating them, and choosing a response.

Reflecting on Thoughts, Feelings, and Behaviors with Self-Talk

Challenging your thoughts or behaviors occurs through the process of self-talk. *Self-talk* is all the things you say to yourself throughout your daily activities, such as "We are out of bananas. I need to stop at the store and get more." Or, in response to a problem, "How am I going to solve this? What do I need to do first?" This silent inner speech is not "talking to yourself" in a literal sense, although sometimes (depending on the person) it is expressed out loud. Everyone engages in self-talk, so doing so is not a sign of being crazy.

You can use self-talk to reflect on your thoughts (subjective) and your feelings (objective); seek to understand the connection; and, with the feedback, make a change in the direction of your goal, purpose, or mission. The idea is to stop your feelings, thoughts, and behaviors from getting in the way of achieving your desired outcome and to use your EQ to actually move you further ahead. The more skilled you are at self-awareness and self-management (components of emotional intelligence), the closer you can come to acting in line with your goals and achieving your desired outcome.

Consider a common job search situation and the possible thoughts, feelings, and behaviors related to the situation:

Situation: You receive a letter in the mail stating that the position that you interviewed for has been filled and thanking you for your application.

Feelings: You feel sad, angry, hopeless, despairing, and depressed.

Bodily cues: Your heart beats faster. You feel your blood pressure rising. Your head starts hurting.

Thoughts: "I did not get this job, which was my dream job, and I likely won't find another one like it. I did not get what I wanted. I will not be happy."

Behaviors: You sleep and eat more; act restless; and remain idle, scattered, and disorganized due to lack of energy, direction, motivation, and confidence.

What can you change here? The situation is what it is, so let's start with your thoughts in response to the situation. You can challenge your thinking, which will change your feelings and hopefully lead to new and more-productive behaviors:

New thoughts: "I did not get this job, which I really wanted. It was the closest I have come to obtaining my dream job. It is unfortunate because I am ready to find a job already. This job search has been quite challenging, but I am closer than I have ever been to getting what I want. I am confident that I have the right skills and experience, and I am going to keep working to find the right opportunity."

New feelings: You still feel sadness about the loss. Yet you also feel somewhat hopeful and optimistic. You are determined and self-confident.

New bodily cues: Your muscles relax. You take some deep breaths or release a big sigh. Your headache starts to dissipate.

New behaviors: You decide to take a day to overcome the sadness and loss of the opportunity. You start the next day evaluating your job search strategy, pushing yourself to follow up with networking calls, and seeking support and ideas from friends.

With these changes, you will feel more satisfied, and you will be more effective and productive.

EQ EXERCISE: IMPROVE THE FEELING-THOUGHT-BEHAVIOR CONNECTION

Respond to the following statements and questions in the space provided.

1. Describe a situation over the past week related to your job search. Pick one in which you had strong feelings.

_____

_____

_____

2. What thoughts were you having at the time?

_____

_____

_____

3. What were you feeling? Circle your feelings on the list of feeling words or write in your own. Rate how strong the feelings were for you on a scale of 1 to 10 (10 being the strongest).

___ Happy	___ Anxious	___ Exhausted
___ Sad	___ Surprised	___ Ashamed
___ Angry	___ Depressed	___ Overwhelmed
___ Scared	___ Confused	___ Hopeful
___ Frustrated	___ Disappointed	___ Shy
___ Embarrassed	___ Confident	___ Bored

4. Write down any physical signs you experienced at the time, such as a headache or a pounding heart. Which were you aware of first, your thoughts or the physical signs in your body?

_____

_____

_____

5. How did you behave in the situation?

_____

_____

_____

(continued)

(continued)

6. Look at what you wrote for question 2. Were the thoughts negative or pessimistic in nature? If so, what would have been a more positive thought?

   _____

   _____

   _____

7. If you were to replace the negative thought with the positive one, how would this change your emotion?

   _____

   _____

   _____

8. Would your new thoughts/feelings lead you to take a different action? If so, describe the action.

   _____

   _____

   _____

   _____

EQ EXERCISE: KEEP A DAILY JOURNAL OR LOG

To become better skilled at thought-feeling-behavior connections, keep a daily journal and write down the situation, your thoughts, your feelings, and your behavior at the time of the event. Over time, you will see connections and maybe some themes or patterns. You will become quicker at making connections in your head without writing them down. You will also become more aware of them in the moment instead of just during reflection. Here is an entry to get you started:

1. Describe the job search situation:

   _____

2. How did you feel in the situation? What bodily cues were you aware of at the time?

_____

3. What were the thoughts going through your mind at that time?

_____

4. How did you respond?

_____

5. What was effective about your response?

_____

6. What was not effective about your response?

_____

7. What can you change or do differently next time?

_____

_____

_____

In the first exercise, you were asked to describe your thoughts in the situation and then to list feelings. In the journal entry, you were asked to write down your feelings and then look at your thoughts. You can also start the process with a look at your behavior. Step back, focus on your actions, and then look at what led you to act that way. Ask yourself, what were the thoughts and feelings you had at that time? Begin at the point in the EQ Connection Triangle that you are most aware of.

Once you amplify your awareness of your thought-feeling-behavior connection, you can work to change your thoughts and behavior to become more productive and more in line with where you want to go. Again, you cannot directly change your feelings. However, you can change your thoughts or behavior to lessen the intensity of the emotion that you are experiencing. For example, counting to 10 before responding is an action you take while you tell yourself to calm down. You are trying to process the thoughts you are having very quickly. When you take deep breaths while counting, you are letting oxygen flow into your body, relaxing your muscles, and giving yourself time to focus on the thoughts that are creating the intense emotion. When you distract yourself and force yourself to think about something different, you are creating new thoughts and feelings. This brings about a decrease in your emotional intensity, because you are no longer focused or obsessing on it.

The goal with self-talk is to be as realistic as possible. But you can choose to face reality in either a positive or negative way. Negative self-talk prevents you from solving problems and responding to challenges; it blocks you from your desired outcome. Positive self-talk focuses on reaching your goal; it provides hopefulness and releases energy to move you forward.

EMOTIONAL INTELLIGENCE IN ACTION

Jamal arrives right on time for his second interview for an account management position in an office equipment and supply company. The receptionist tells him to have a seat, and Mr. Brown will be right with him. Fifteen minutes later, the receptionist tells Jamal that Mr. Brown apologizes for being late, but he has to deal with an urgent matter first and that he will be with him shortly. After half an hour, Jamal begins feeling angry that he has had to wait. Jamal reflects on his thought, "Mr. Brown doesn't think this interview, and thus me, is very important." He uses his EQ to stop this negative thinking and challenge it, turning it to a more positive thought with self-talk. He thinks, "Mr. Brown has some urgent matter, and I need to be patient. I can remember when I was running late for meetings and felt bad for keeping people waiting and for being late." Jamal starts feeling less angry as a result of focusing on this positive thought and feels calmer and lighter.

Mr. Brown walks into the lobby and greets Jamal, saying he is very sorry about making him wait so long. Jamal shows his emotional intelligence with his response, "I can remember having those kinds of days. Something would always come up at the last minute to pull the whole day off track." Mr. Brown laughs and agrees. He seems relaxed and ready to talk with Jamal. Now that Jamal is no longer angry, he is less likely to say or do something in the interview that will cost him the job.

Challenging Destructive Thoughts

Psychologist Albert Ellis presented the idea that people develop irrational beliefs that interfere with healthy functioning. These beliefs are forms of distorted or inaccurate thinking because they are not fully supported by reality. They are not logical thoughts because they are often based on false assumptions.

How do you challenge these thoughts so as to arrive at different feelings and thus take different actions? The following sections provide examples of how to handle the most common types of distorted thinking and strategies for ensuring that you maintain a realistic view of your job search situation.

Recognizing Distorted Thinking

There are some common themes of thoughts that can lead to unhappy feelings and unproductive behavior. David Burns shares common themes of this kind of distorted thinking in his book, *Feeling Good: The New Mood Therapy*. In the following sections, I show examples of some of the common themes he mentions and provide more-realistic or -positive thoughts that challenge the destructive ones. The idea is that if you change destructive thoughts to more-realistic thoughts, you will feel more hopeful and more motivated to continue on in your job search and overcome the obstacle in front of you instead of staying in a mindset that leads you to feel and act defeated.

Jumping to Conclusions or Making Assumptions

When you do not consider all the facts or when you do not have all the information, you might make false assumptions, as shown in the following examples.

Destructive thought:

> *"I must get a job by next month or I will be in such poor financial shape that I don't think I'll ever get out of the hole."*

Challenge:

> *"I would like to get a job by the end of next month. It would work out great from a financial perspective. If I don't, I'll be okay. I may have to borrow money and then work that much harder to catch up, but I can do it."*

Destructive thought:

> *"The Jones Company won't call me for an interview. I don't have any pull to get into that company."*

Challenge:

"I know that knowing someone helps you to get in the door of The Jones Company. I have some ideas on how I can possibly get around that. One is to join the American Marketing Association, because I know some of their key marketing executives attend those meetings."

Destructive thought:

"If I don't get this job offer, I will never get my dream job."

Challenge:

"I will be upset and disappointed if I do not get this job. However, I choose not to give up on finding a job in this area."

Discrediting Yourself

When you focus on the negative and do not take into account positive factors or the reality of the situation, you set yourself up for destructive thinking, as shown in the following examples.

Destructive thought:

"I felt a great connection with the interviewer, but I must be reading things all wrong because I didn't get the job. I don't know what to think anymore."

Challenge:

"I am disappointed I did not get the job. Even though I had a good connection with the interviewer, there must have been a more skilled candidate. Because I had a good rapport with the interviewer, I think I will follow up with him to see if he can give me any feedback on my qualifications."

Destructive thought:

"I have never been asked to leave a company before. I have always been wanted by each company I have worked for. I guess I was fooling everybody up until now. I don't have what it takes."

Challenge:

"I am an excellent engineer, and I have the performance evaluations from several managers to support this statement. The company has been losing money each quarter over the past two years. A reorganization to become more profitable was bound to happen, and my job was affected like so many others."

Blaming Yourself

Believing you are the total cause of a bad event can be irrational, as shown in the following examples.

Destructive thought:

"I did not get a raise this year. I know it is because I did not do a good job. With the limited funds, there are too many others that deserve it more than I do."

Challenge:

"I am disappointed that I did not get a raise. I know that not everyone will get a raise due to the company's financial situation. I am going to ask my boss what areas I need to improve on so that I can be considered for a raise next year."

Destructive thought:

"They did not return my phone call or respond to my e-mail messages. I know they don't think I am a good candidate for the job."

Challenge:

"I feel frustrated when I don't receive a response from others. When I don't hear anything, I feel further away from my goal of landing a job. However, even though I haven't heard back from them, it does not mean that I am not being considered. I have not received a rejection letter. Maybe the decision maker is away. I need to stay positive until I know for sure."

Should or Must Statements

Should or Must statements are the rules you tell yourself that often are very critical of yourself and others, such as the following:

Destructive thought:

> *"I really blew that interview. I should have said _____ instead of _____, and now I look like an idiot."*

Challenge:

> *"I did not respond as well as I wanted to. I was nervous. I am still a capable person. Next time I will say _____."*

Destructive thought:

> *"I should send my resume to 500 companies this week, or I am not doing a good job on my job search."*

Challenge:

> *"I am a hard worker, and I am working hard on this job search. I would like to send out as many resumes as possible this week. My goal is to send 20 resumes and cover letters, and if I can do more, than that will be like the icing on the cake."*

Destructive thought:

> *"I must get accepted into this MBA program, or I will not be happy."*

Challenge:

> *"I hope to be accepted into the MBA program. If I do not get in, I will be disappointed and sad. However, I am not giving up. I will apply again in the fall. I will add community service to my application by getting involved now in a charity organization."*

All-or-Nothing Thinking, Always or Never Statements

Like the Should or Must statements, Always or Never statements are rules that you establish for yourself. The difference is that they are extreme. Perfectionism often comes into play. As shown in the following examples, you can challenge these statements easily because they are not completely accurate. Rarely is something so black and white!

Destructive thought:

"I didn't get the job because the interviewer was a jerk!"

Challenge:

"The interviewer was hard to connect with, and I may not get the job, but I have no control over that. At least I was aware of the situation, and I did my best to connect with the interviewer. I am going to reflect on the interview to see what I could have done differently to make a connection. I do feel good that I was qualified for the position based on my experience."

Destructive thought:

"I always do badly in interviews."

Challenge:

"Interviews are difficult for me. I have to find a way to get better at them. I do not want it to stop me from landing the job I want. I am going to get some help from a career coach with this issue."

Destructive thought:

"This was the perfect job for me. I don't know how the company will get by without me. I will never find another job that I like as well or am as skilled at as this one."

Challenge:

"I liked this job a lot, but it did have a 45-minute commute. I know that everyone is replaceable. Hopefully, I can find another job that I enjoy with half the commute time. That would be great."

Thinking Realistically

The goal (and challenge) is to assess the situation as accurately and objectively as possible. You gather data by using all your senses and by what you intuitively feel. You also assign thoughts to the data coming in. You then make decisions based on your interpretation of the data. Your interpretations could be right, or they could be wrong. You need to examine your interpretations by asking yourself whether they are accurate. You can also seek out more information or check out your ideas with others.

To make accurate interpretations and assess situations realistically, use these guidelines:

- Be honest with yourself. Try to see things as they really are.

- Make sure that you have all the data you need to make a good decision, and look at that data objectively and carefully. Gather more data from others and your surroundings if needed.

- Evaluate the pros and cons to each side.

- Ask yourself whether you are refusing to consider some of the data because it is uncomfortable to deal with.

- Be on the lookout for destructive thought processes, such as all-or-nothing thinking and others mentioned earlier in the chapter.

- Accept the fact you are unique. Do not compare yourself to others. There is only one you! You have strengths and weaknesses like everyone else. No one is perfect.

- Keep your emotions in check. If you are depressed or angry, manage the emotion so you do not keep—and thus show—a negative image of yourself.

- Sometimes perceptions become extremely distorted due to traumatic childhood experiences or medical conditions. Professional help is needed in this case.

Shaping Thoughts with Creative Visualization

Creative visualization, as defined by Mary Ballou in her book, *Psychological Interventions: A Guide to Strategies,* refers to the practice of seeking to affect the outer world via changing one's thoughts. It is positive thinking done in an effort to shape your perception and beliefs, which drives you closer to making your goal a reality.

Athletes use creative visualization all the time. They imagine what the experience of winning is like. They visualize the path to get there. They picture the obstacles along the way and how to overcome each obstacle. They then recreate those thoughts, images, perceptions as they work toward achieving the goal.

In visualization, you form a mental picture of the experience of achieving your goal. By doing this, you are changing your perception to reflect on success in the future and what it looks and feels like. As you experience this visualization, your self-talk becomes "I can do this. I am going to do this." In a virtual sense, you experience the success of achieving the goal and the related feelings of pride and excitement. This positive energy and these connections then affect your energy in the present and motivate you to move forward. On the other hand, if you visualize failing at your goal, and you use negative self-talk, such as, "I am a failure. I cannot do this," you will experience feelings of defeat, weakness, and sadness. This experience can and will zap your energy and drive.

To stay positive during the job search, visualize success! Visualize success in your networking interactions. Visualize success in the upcoming interview. Visualize success in your new job.

EQ EXERCISE: USE VISUALIZATION IN THE JOB SEARCH

Pick a quiet place to reflect. Get into a comfortable position. Allow yourself to relax. Relax your body and your mind. Let go of any thoughts you are currently having. Put them away on a shelf somewhere in your mind. Store them to think about another time.

Next, picture yourself achieving a goal. Allow yourself to picture as many details as possible. Use your senses fully. What do you see around you? What do you hear? What are you touching or sensing? What do you smell or taste?

Focus on your experience in this moment. How are you feeling? Describe it. What are some of the thoughts going through your mind as you experience the moment? Allow yourself to reflect and imagine all the obstacles that you overcame to get to this point. Allow yourself to sense the person you are and have become.

Lastly, bring yourself out of the moment, slowly back to the quiet place in which you have been doing this reflection exercise. Write down this experience. Try to put into words the thoughts and feelings you experienced. Do you feel and think you can attain this goal? Are you ready to take action to reach this goal? How can you take steps to overcome the obstacles? Of course, visualization alone is not going to make your goal a reality, but for many people it is an effective tool to move them closer to success.

Changing Behavior First

So far in this chapter, I have focused on thoughts and how changing them changes your emotions. But thoughts are only one part of the EQ Connection Triangle. You also can change your behavior, which then leads to new thoughts and thus a change in your emotions. Instead of initiating change by challenging your thinking, you can take action and direct your behavior toward your desired outcome or ultimate goal.

Suppose you come home from work and you are deciding whether to take a walk or sit on the couch and watch TV. You don't feel like taking a walk; you feel tired. You think about the fact that taking a walk will put you more in line with your desired outcome, which is to be healthy and to feel good. You also think about the hassle of changing into comfortable clothes in order to go for a walk. But you push yourself to put on your tennis shoes, go outside, and take the walk (behavior). As you walk, you reflect, "It is nice to see the sun today. It feels refreshing to have the cool breeze on my face." These new sensations help you to feel good, more calm and peaceful. You return from your walk feeling better. You achieved something that was in line with the outcome you desired, to feel better and to be healthy. The behavior affected your thoughts, which ultimately affected your emotions.

Behaving as if you expect job success is very important. You have to continue to do all the actions that go with a job search—such as sending out resumes, networking, or doing research—to be successful. There will be times when you do not feel like doing it or you tell yourself negative things that justify your inaction. Giving in to these feelings and thoughts does not get you any closer to your goal of landing a job.

Monitoring and Managing Your Emotions

Emotions are a part of life. The premise behind emotional intelligence is to learn how to recognize your emotions and deal with them effectively so they do not get in the way of your desired outcome or goal. The alternative is to simply let your emotions run wild, which can be dangerous. In the book *Emotional Intelligence,* author Daniel Goleman discusses the process of "emotional hijacking," which occurs when you let your emotions overwhelm you and you become ineffective in reaching your desired outcome. Instead of getting closer to what you want, you move further away.

Anxiety is one potentially overwhelming emotion. If you allow it to become too high during a job interview, you will not be able to talk clearly and communicate your message. The interviewer will be more aware of your anxiety than your answers. Yet if you ignore all of your anxiousness, you might seem overconfident and boastful and come across as a know-it-all.

Anger is another emotion that can easily become overwhelming. For example, you are in a job interview, and the interviewer seems very rude. He doesn't shake your hand when you first meet, and he then interrupts you several times when you speak. You might start to feel angry in response to the interviewer's behavior. The interviewer goes on to question whether your background would really work for the position you are applying for. Now you really start to feel uncomfortable and even angrier because you are thinking that he does not value you nor your experience. You are thinking that you are here to get the job, and this interviewer seems to have ruled you out before he has even given you a chance! You now have a choice on how to respond. You might respond angrily, defensively, and possibly critically by telling the interviewer that he does not understand what you have to offer. Will this response get you what you ultimately want? No. He will likely not hire you, and you will not achieve your goal of getting the job offer.

A different way to respond to this situation is to use your emotional intelligence. You become aware of your angry feelings during the interview and of the thoughts connected with those angry feelings. Using self-talk, you say to yourself, "this interviewer is not responding to me in a positive way." You challenge your thought of being angry at the interviewer and say to yourself, "it is not me that is the issue here. I know I have the skills and experience, and the company has called me for an interview based on my resume." You accept that the interviewer is not supportive of you for this position for whatever reason. You decide to handle yourself positively and continue to be respectful. Using your self-talk to challenge your thoughts, thus reducing your anger, allows you to refocus on what you want—a connection with this interviewer. Ultimately you want the job offer, and you have to do all that you can do to make this happen. Even though he may not hire you in the end, you did not burn the bridge by being disrespectful to him. What if the interviewer was purposely trying to test your reaction and assess how you manage yourself? What if he intentionally created the same scenario with all of the applicants?

Another possible way to respond using your EQ is to respond in an understanding and empathic way. You think about the interviewer's perspective and use self-talk to try not to personalize the situation. Instead of responding back negatively and angrily, you stay calm, keep emotions in check, and politely ask, "What on my resume appealed to you or to those who decided I should come in for an interview?" The interviewer can then step back from his current stance and answer the question. He may say that his two colleagues liked your strong management skills, but that he was looking for more of a knowledge expert.

Being empathic, you can ask more questions about his views and show that you value his perspective. You respond to his concerns and inform him of the skills and strategies you can offer to join him in his mission. You say that you respect his decision, but state that you hope he will consider you for the position. By being emotionally intelligent, you are able to pick up on the idea that the interviewer is already feeling outnumbered by his two colleagues who want a strong manager. So you join with him instead of responding defensively. Are you closer to getting another interview? I think so.

Emotions can overwhelm you if you repeatedly allow them to get in the way. Therefore, you need to monitor your emotions not only in the moment, but also over time. Emotions when held over long periods of time, often labeled as moods, have long-ranging effects. If you do not stop to reflect on your feelings and thoughts on a regular basis, you are not managing them. They can build, and over time, even without realizing it, you can begin to feel helpless, as if nothing you do is working. You become immobilized. You do not know how to respond, and you do not move forward. Essentially, you stop taking action.

Imagine a job seeker who gets four rejection letters during a two-week period from companies that he was very interested in. These events occur three months into his job search when he is really starting to feel financial stresses and worry about paying the bills. His emotions and thoughts are all about despair and failure, and thus he cannot move himself to take action. He feels no energy, no motivation, and no drive. He can continue to ignore his emotions, or he can use his emotional intelligence. He can change this cycle by awareness and management of his thoughts, feelings, and behaviors. Being able to make this type of change takes time and practice.

Note that some individuals may experience this helplessness in a severe form such as depression. If you suspect depression is in play, it needs to be diagnosed and treated medically through a doctor. Depression is a biological condition that needs medical intervention first and then psychological intervention through counseling second in order for the individual to function most effectively. Once you are in a stable form of functioning, you can work on developing your emotional intelligence competencies.

Chapter Reflections

Emotional intelligence is the process of reflecting on the connections between your thoughts, feelings, and behaviors and using the information to manage yourself and others in the direction of your goal or desired outcome.

Emotional intelligence also has a biological basis. You develop emotional intelligence by incorporating data and making connections between the limbic system, the emotional part of the brain, and the neocortex, the rational part of the brain. The process of incorporating new data and learning into existing circuitry extends and strengthens neural pathways.

Making these connections in the brain begins with your self-awareness of the interplay between your thoughts, feelings, and behaviors. The EQ Connection Triangle is a way of looking at these relationships. You reflect on and identify these connections and then change one of them, which affects the others in return and moves you toward your goals and desired outcomes. Reflection and self-talk are the tools for monitoring and changing the thought-feeling-behavior connections.

Changing your thoughts involves challenging the distorted thinking and assessing the situation accurately. Changing your behavior involves acting as if you are achieving your goal, and then letting thoughts and emotions change as a result. Remember, you cannot directly change an emotion. It is automatic. You lessen its intensity only through changing the related thoughts and behaviors first. Ignoring your emotions will only produce more problems and lead you further away from your desired goal or outcome. To manage emotions effectively, you monitor them in the moment and over time through the process of reflection and self-talk.

PART II

Applying Emotional Intelligence Skills for Job Search Success

Part II reviews each core skill area of emotional intelligence:

- Chapter 3, "Self-Awareness: Know Who You Are for a True Job Search Edge," explains the skills of emotion identification, accurate self-assessment, and self-confidence. As you might remember from the Introduction, these skills are particularly important during stage I (managing emotions/self-assessment) and stage III (targeting specific jobs and careers) of the career transition process.

- Chapter 4, "Self-Management: Find Focus and Maintain Motivation," explains the skills of self-control, adaptability, stress management, and motivation/optimism. These skills are particularly important during stage IV (interviewing for positions) of the career transition process.

- Chapter 5, "Social Awareness: Empathize with Employers and Make the Most of Opportunities," explains the skills of empathy, reality testing, and social responsibility. These skills are particularly important during stage II (exploring career options) and stage III (targeting specific jobs and careers) of the career transition process.

- Chapter 6, "Social Skills: Communicate and Collaborate to Succeed in the Job Search," explains the skills of trust and honesty, communication and assertiveness, cooperation and collaboration, conflict management and negotiation, and influence on and development of others. These skills are particularly important during stage IV (interviewing for positions) and stage V (negotiating and accepting a job offer) of the career transition process.

Each chapter provides real-world examples of these skills at work in a job search situation and exercises to help you develop each skill. These chapters also explain how to apply these EQ skills to your career goals: finding the right career, selecting the right job, and getting the job offer. To help you visualize each EQ skill, I end these chapters by describing role models who display a high amount of that skill.

CHAPTER 3

Self-Awareness: Know Who You Are for a True Job Search Edge

Self-awareness is simply being able to reflect on your thoughts, feelings, and behaviors and use this information to guide you. It is the first of the four large skill sets that make up emotional intelligence, and it is the skill set upon which all the other EQ skills are built. It is composed of the following three skills:

- Emotion identification
- Accurate self-assessment
- Self-confidence

In this chapter, you will learn how to become more self-aware by building these skills and applying them in your job search.

The Cornerstone of Job Search Success: Emotion Identification

Emotion identification involves being aware of your feelings and linking them to the thoughts that contribute to that feeling. Bodily cues such as a sick feeling in your stomach can tell you that you are upset about something. Understanding what is causing the feeling that you are experiencing and then taking and using this information to guide your response in an appropriate and effective way is emotion identification.

EMOTIONAL INTELLIGENCE IN ACTION

Scott really needs a job because of his poor financial situation. After a couple of months of looking, he finally has a job interview scheduled. He thinks, "I have to get this job. Everything is riding on how I do in this interview. If I lose this

(continued)

(continued)

opportunity, I don't know what I am going to do." In the days leading up to the interview, his stomach seems to hurt all the time, so he stops eating regularly.

When a day or two has passed, Scott recognizes that he has had that type of pain before when he was worried about something important. He reflects on this physical cue and his feelings of nervousness and on what he has been saying to himself. He realizes that he needs to stop the negative thinking and change it to more-positive thoughts, such as, "I would like this job, and I am going to do my best. If I do not get the offer, I will stay optimistic and keep on working on my next opportunity." He also decides to make himself eat better so that he can feel physically better now and in the interview.

Scott uses his awareness of his emotions and thoughts and observes how they are negatively affecting his job search. He manages them by changing his negative thoughts to more-positive ones, which in turn drives his behavior in the direction of his goal of getting a job.

People experience emotions at different levels of intensity. Some respond to a rejection letter with hours of sobbing and remain inactive on the job search for days. Others, in response to same event, may communicate feelings of disappointment, but follow such communication with optimistic statements, such as "the right job will come," and quickly return to searching for job leads and preparing for the next interview. If your feelings affect your performance and relationships, it is to your advantage to identify them correctly so you can move in a positive direction.

EQ EXERCISE: IDENTIFY JOB SEARCH EMOTIONS

Identifying your emotions is being true and honest to yourself. Identifying emotions takes time and effort, but it becomes quicker and easier with practice. If you want to incorporate this skill into your daily life, you are ready to take these steps:

1. Feelings are messages telling us something, so be aware of your feelings at all times. Ask yourself, "What am I feeling now?" Label your feelings with words such as the following:

Happy	Anxious	Exhausted
Sad	Surprised	Ashamed

Angry	Depressed	Overwhelmed
Scared	Confused	Hopeful
Frustrated	Disappointed	Shy
Embarrassed	Confident	Bored

2. Note the physical signs that go along with these feelings.

3. Reflect on your thoughts and identify how they connect to your feelings.

4. Link your feelings, thoughts, and behaviors during your job search by keeping a journal and reviewing these connections.

As you review your journal, think about job search events that trigger specific feelings. Brace yourself to be ready to deal with those triggers when they pop up. For example, how do you feel after a full day of no one returning your phone calls or e-mail messages? Likely you feel discouraged and possibly angry. First be aware of the feeling and search your thoughts about the situation. You may be thinking that others don't see the importance of your e-mail or phone calls, and you may feel rejected or hurt. Challenge your thoughts. Your job search is extremely important to you, and timing is critical. However, the reality is that your job search is not a priority to others. When you hear back from them, be polite and respectful. Be understanding of their time, and thank them for their responses when they come.

EQ EXERCISE: VENT FEELINGS AND CHANGE NEGATIVE THOUGHTS

As you become more aware of your feelings and thoughts, pay particular attention to the negative ones. Think about how you can vent negative feelings, such as anger and jealousy, in order to move on in your job search and be more constructive. For example, when you are feeling angry, you might call and talk to a friend and ask for her or his thoughts about the situation.

(continued)

(continued)

Complete the following sentences:

When I am feeling angry, I will…

_____

When I am feeling discouraged, I will…

_____

When I am feeling rejected, I will…

_____

When I am feeling jealous, I will…

_____

When you have negative thoughts, ask yourself, "How can I think more positively in this situation?" For practice, change these negative thoughts to positive ones:

If I am not good at something, I should just give up.

_____

No one is calling me for an interview, so I must lack skills.

_____

My resume shows that I am nothing special. Many people can do what I do.

_____

I am bad at interviewing, so I will do terrible in this interview.

_____

The company let me go, so I must be a bad worker.

_____

I will never find a good-paying job.

_____

EMOTIONAL IDENTIFICATION IN ACTION

Aisha learned today that she did not get the job offer from Company ABC that she interviewed for last week. She feels sad, disappointed, and rejected. She starts thinking that she will never find a job and that she does not have the skills needed to get a good-paying job. In the middle of thinking these negative thoughts, Aisha stops to reflect and realizes that she is making herself feel worse. She uses her self-awareness to acknowledge and accept her sadness at the loss of the potential offer, but tells herself that she needs to stop her negative thinking and change her ideas to positive ones, such as "I will get a job," and "I do have skills, but I am going to attend a computer certification class to enhance my skills and improve my confidence." As she focuses on these positive thoughts, she feels more hopeful and confident that she will eventually get a job. These positive thoughts and feelings will drive her to take more-positive actions in her job search.

Identifying Beliefs and Values

In Chapter 2, you learned that to fully use your emotional intelligence, you not only need to reflect on your thoughts and feelings in the moment, but also reflect back over time on your past emotions and thoughts and use this information to guide your behavior. When you reflect on past emotions, patterns emerge, and these patterns indicate what your beliefs and values are.

Beliefs are the thoughts that guide your behavior and are connected to the choices you make in how you live your life. Emotions can create a presence within you over time and become connected to your beliefs. *Values* can be viewed as this comprehensive presence within you that is composed of your emotions and thoughts and becomes a part of your life perspective, driving your actions and influencing your decisions. Values drive your behaviors and decisions on a daily basis. Basically, values are beliefs that become emotionally charged and are given importance and priority by you.

Knowing what your beliefs and values are can help you make better decisions, which can lead to greater life satisfaction. Yet the importance of values and beliefs in the decision-making process is often overlooked. In the book *Emotional Intelligence: Why It Can Matter More Than IQ*, author

Daniel Goleman makes a strong case for how feelings play an important role in the small and large decisions that you make every day. His message is that you need both your rational thoughts in conjunction with your gut feelings and emotional wisdom from your past experiences to guide you in your decision making.

In Chapter 2, you learned how to challenge beliefs that may be serving as obstacles to your goals. Sometimes you can come up with thoughts that are not fully rational or reality based. For example, I coached a candidate who was undecided about her career direction after completing her bachelor's degree in Psychology. She was extremely bright and talented and had many resources within her reach. Through our coaching work, she became aware of how she felt compelled to follow a medical research career in order to find a cure for a disease that affected her brother. She felt loyal and committed to him and wanted to improve his and others' lives who were struggling with this disease. However, she realized that she had other interests that she also wanted to explore. Through coaching, she became aware or conscious of the ideas that she was telling herself, such as "I should be a medical researcher," and "If I don't go into medicine, I will be letting down my brother and family." I challenged her word *should*. I asked, "Who says you should?" I reminded her that she was in charge of her life and the decisions that she made. Hopefully her family would want what was best for her and would support her no matter what decision she made.

In addition to beliefs, values were involved in this dilemma. She valued her family relationships and helping others, as well as her independence and freedom of choice. The goal is to identify your values and how they affect your decisions. When you make a decision that is in line with your values, you feel satisfied. When you are in a situation that conflicts with your values, you are likely to feel dissatisfied, uncomfortable, or unhappy.

For example, work/life balance has always been a strong value for me. When my work becomes overwhelming, and it starts taking my weekday evenings and weekends to catch up, I start to resent that work is crowding in my personal and family time, which is important to me. So I access my awareness of my feelings and make a change to rebalance myself and thus create more personal time and balance. I may have to do this by cutting back on my hours (which I am also aware has consequences) or having a talk about priorities with my manager so as to refocus my energy and time.

EMOTIONAL INTELLIGENCE IN ACTION

Nathan has worked for a family business for some time and has come to realize that not being a member of the family has stopped him from advancing. When high-level positions become available, they are always filled with family members. He feels frustrated and angry because he has invested time, loyalty, and commitment to the business and has not received any increased income or status in return. After reflecting on what is important to him, he realizes that his values of achievement, financial gain, recognition, and status were not being fulfilled in this job. He decided to make a decision to leave the business in order to find a job more in line with his values, which would hopefully make him happier. He was able to be aware of his frustration and could identify his values and how this job conflicted with them. In becoming more self-aware, he was able to make a change and look for a job that was more in line with his values, hopefully leading to happiness and job satisfaction.

EQ EXERCISE: IDENTIFY YOUR VALUES

Indicate the 10 values that are most important to you at this time in your life by circling them in the following list or writing in your own:

Money	Stability	Prestige	Achievement
Adventure	Power	Helping others	Knowledge
Creativity	Passion	Interests	Pleasure
Independence	Affection	Caring	Beauty
Challenge	Collaboration	Community	Competition
Contribution	Power	Family	Travel
Leadership	Friendship	Partnership	Freedom
Harmony	Health	Honesty	Humor
Work/life balance	Spirituality	Stability	Growth

(continued)

(continued)

Helping society	Tradition	Leisure	Location
Loyalty	Success	Peace	Productivity
Recognition	Romance	Risk-taking	Self-expression
Service	Excitement	_____	_____
_____	_____	_____	_____

Look at the values that you circled. Some fit together, such as leisure and pleasure, and can be grouped together. Write your groupings here:

Value Groupings

_____

_____

_____

Of these values, which are most important to you? Write your five most important values in the following space. You will want to look for these in your next job position or career choice.

My Top Five Values

1. _____

2. _____

3. _____

4. _____

5. _____

Using Emotion Identification to Choose a Career

As you have learned, emotion identification is an important part of making decisions. For example, if you were a high school student selecting a college, you would have to know the requirements you need in a college, such as public or private, small or large, or rural or suburban. You would base your decision not only on how a college met your criteria, but also on the feeling you have when you are on the college campus. Visiting the campus allows you to experience the emotions you feel while in the environment. You can experience your reactions to the setting and to the kinds of people that you meet. You can compare it to your past experiences in similar settings. Awareness in the moment of how you are feeling, along with all the other cognitive facts and information, should lead you to a college that suits you.

When you choose a career, you need to take your feelings into account as well as your abilities. Suppose you are good at math. You decide that you should be a statistician because statisticians work with numbers. Besides, your father and grandfather were statisticians. Statisticians also work alone for significant periods of time, which was fine for Dad and Gramps because they were loners. However, you, being self-aware, know that you are an outgoing person who likes to be around people most of the time. You think about past experiences and realize that when you have been cooped up at a desk for a couple hours, working on numbers, you felt drained and needed to seek out interaction with others. This self-awareness may lead you to question the career of a statistician and lean toward being a math teacher instead. As a math teacher, you can enjoy your love of numbers while you interact with students.

Making a career choice entails being honest with yourself and with what you know about a career. Think of professionals in those occupations that you are considering. Can you picture yourself doing what they do? What are your thoughts and feelings about what they do in their job? You can gather information talking to various professionals and checking out their perspectives. (Learning about careers and job responsibilities to help you match yourself to a career or job involves your social awareness and will be reviewed in Chapter 5.) Reflect on your thoughts and feelings about a career and the courses you would have to pass to be qualified for that career. Using self-talk, ask yourself whether this would be the right career choice for you. Write down your thoughts. Make a pros-and-cons list. Make sure you have looked at the facts and your feelings before you make a decision.

Using Emotion Identification to Find the Right Job

Once you have decided on a career or job and completed the necessary training and education, you look for the right position to apply to. For example, what industry do you want to work in? What kinds of companies are you most interested in working for? You want to use all of the information at your disposal to make a good decision. This information includes your thoughts about the company and your feelings in the interview, as well as information that you gathered from the job description and through research on the company. Identifying your emotions and thoughts while you are at the company for an interview will give you much information about whether this is the right job to pursue. Identifying your feelings when you are in the environment and meeting people who work there will help you determine whether it feels comfortable and appealing to you.

Using Emotion Identification to Get the Job Offer

Focus on your feelings during an interview and use your awareness of them and your related thoughts to manage yourself appropriately. For example, if you are waiting in an office lobby before an important interview and you notice that your voice tone has become broken and your heart is pounding, you can use your emotion identification skill to conclude that you are anxious. A certain amount of anxiety is normal and actually helps put your body on alert. You have important work ahead of you: to perform well in this interview so that you will be offered the job or at least a second interview. To manage your anxiety, you might take a couple of deep breaths, or you may choose to tell the interviewer, "As you can tell by the tone of my voice, I am nervous. I really want to do a good job in this interview because I would like to work for your company." A smile and possibly some joint laughter can ease the situation. This type of revelation shows your vulnerability and humanness. You build trust through your genuine sharing of yourself in the moment and show yourself to be emotionally intelligent.

Being aware of the impact that you are having on the interviewer and using this information can guide you to perform more effectively. In the interview, it is important to be aware of yourself but also to monitor the interviewer's emotions, from the nonverbal cues to his responses and behaviors. What are his facial expressions and actions in relation to what you have communicated? If he is listening intently and smiling, you know you are connecting in a good way. You may continue to use your sense of humor because it appears to be having a positive impact. If you notice that the interviewer is distracted or starting to nod off as you answer a question, then your impact is not so good, and you may be boring him. If you are aware of this as it is happening, you can change your tone of voice, for example, and be louder or more enthusiastic. Or you may decide to talk less and ask more questions so the interviewer can talk.

When you are in the interview, perform as if you definitely want the job. After the interview, you can reflect on the job, interviewer, and company and decide whether you really want the job if it is offered to you. You will make a good decision if you have fully and honestly reflected on your thoughts and feelings from your experiences.

Accurate Self-Assessment: Know Your Strengths and Weaknesses for the Job Search

The second skill under the area of self-awareness is accurate self-assessment. Self-assessment involves being aware of your strengths and weaknesses and using that information to help you in your job search. Strengths can help propel you in a positive direction toward your goals. Finding jobs in which you can use your strengths will place you at an advantage. You will like what you are doing and will be very skilled and successful in doing that work. You want to be aware of weaknesses so that you can either steer away from jobs that entail those skills or you can decide whether you want to develop those weak areas to be more successful in that kind of job.

Be honest with yourself as you sort out what you are good at and what you are not good at. Doing an accurate self-assessment takes courage. Focusing on your weaknesses is difficult. For example, let's say you were extremely talkative in an interview. The person interviewing you makes a comment that he was not able to ask several questions because you had some very long answers. As you leave the interview, you tell yourself (self-talk) that you talked a lot, but this gave the interviewer a lot of information about you.

You are not being honest with yourself. The reality is that your talking prevented the interviewer from hearing answers to other important questions because he did not get the chance to ask them. The result is that you will not get called back for a second interview. By using your self-awareness and by being honest, you can admit that you did talk too much. The next step is to forgive yourself, move on, and resolve to talk less in future interviews. What can you do to remind yourself to talk less and answer with shorter, more-effective responses? Try wearing a rubber band on your wrist as a cue to remind you to talk less in the interview.

The more aware you are, the more objectively you can look at your feelings and thoughts and work on accepting them, challenging them, or changing them. The more you can say, "I'm okay, even with my weaknesses and mistakes," the more accepting you can be of yourself and the happier you will be. Also, the greater your awareness of yourself and your behavior in the context of the world around you, the greater the number of choices you have in responding to others in the situation. Greater awareness of your strengths and weaknesses, emotions, beliefs, and values will lead to a more effective job search because you become more aware of what you have to offer and how to handle yourself most effectively in the interview in order to get the job offer.

EMOTIONAL INTELLIGENCE IN ACTION

Raul knows that he is quiet and introverted. He also knows that many people find their next job through networking with people, instead of from a response to an Internet ad. He is aware of his discomfort with networking and accepts it as a weakness and approaches his job search with this in mind.

He decides to do two things. First, he uses his strength of knowledge of computers and information technology to spend time each week searching certain select sites to apply for specific jobs; he also uses Internet networking resources, such as LinkedIn. Second, he decides to work on his weakness by joining a job support focus group to force him to interact with others and gain information about job searching. He feels this group might be a good way to improve his networking skills. He also is aware that he will have to talk more in interviews. To make this easier, he prepares answers to common interview questions. His plan is to share more information, which will force him to talk more in the interview.

When you are aware of your weaknesses, you can manage them in a way that they do not work against you. Like Raul, you can strategize ways to overcome the weaknesses and not let them hinder you in landing the job.

EQ EXERCISE: ASSESS YOUR STRENGTHS AND WEAKNESSES

Self-awareness of strengths, weaknesses, interests, abilities, and skills is a basis for choosing a career, changing jobs, or changing careers. The following are coaching questions designed to help you take an inventory of yourself and clarify your career direction and goals.

List your six biggest career or job-related accomplishments. Also include the result or outcome for your employer.

1. _____

_____

2. _____

_____

3. _____

_____

4. _____

_____

5. _____

_____

6. _____

_____

Think about each of these accomplishments and then write down the skills you used to achieve each one:

1. _____

_____

(continued)

(continued)

2. _____

_____

3. _____

_____

4. _____

_____

5. _____

_____

6. _____

_____

A strength is a skill that you enjoy using. Review the skills you listed and note your top three strengths. Also, give an example of a time you used that strength that is not included in your list of biggest career accomplishments.

1. _____

_____

2. _____

_____

3. _____

_____

Think about the career transition process described in the introduction to this book. How can you fully use your top strengths in your job search activities?

_____

_____

_____

_____

_____

List three weaknesses (these can be the EQ areas that you scored lowest on in the quiz in Chapter 1). How might they hinder a successful job search? Will you work to develop these areas, and, if so, how will you improve them? Or will you try to work around them?

1._____

_____

2._____

_____

3._____

_____

Using Accurate Self-Assessment to Choose a Career

Look at your strengths and weaknesses and decide which careers will let you use your strengths. Keep in mind that you want to choose a career that fits your personality, interests, values, and beliefs in addition to your skills and experience. You want to select a career and job that require the skills and abilities that you enjoy using.

Taking a career assessment helps increase your self-awareness. Career assessments are based on the idea that you will be happiest in a career using skills and abilities that you are good at and enjoy. These assessments match you with occupations by matching your interests with people working in those careers, focusing on people who enjoy the kind of work they are doing. These assessments can be obtained online or by seeking out a career coach or counselor in your area who is trained to give them—and provide accurate feedback. In my coaching work, I use the Strong Interest Inventory and the Myers-Briggs Type Indicator, which are very sound and useful instruments.

Steven Stein and Howard Book in their book, *The EQ Edge: Emotional Intelligence and Your Success,* did research to explore the question, "What does it take to be successful at work?" They tested 4,888 working people in various occupations throughout North America using the EQ-i emotional intelligence assessment. They asked people how successful they believed they were at their jobs. (Keep in mind that this is a self-report measure and comes with limitations, but it can provide useful information.)

Within various occupations, they were able to list the top emotional intelligence traits for differentiating between high and low performers in that occupation. The idea is that people who are most satisfied with their work tend to be those whose emotional skills fit the formula for that work. For example, elementary school teachers scored high in optimism, independence, dealing with stress, and self-regard (generally liking and accepting themselves). Knowing that these are important qualities in teaching can help you decide whether this profession would be a good one for you by asking yourself whether you have these EQ qualities. If these are not strong qualities for you, you may question whether you will truly be happy and successful in that career.

When choosing a career, it is important to check out your career choice with others and be honest with yourself. If you know you do not have the cognitive intelligence to master the college science courses that are needed to complete a degree to be an astronaut, it is best to let go of this desire and look at another option that is more in line with your skills. Trying to attain something that is realistically beyond your reach can frustrate you and lead to feelings of low self-esteem and low self-worth. You can avoid these feelings with accurate self-assessment.

EQ EXERCISE: TARGET THE RIGHT CAREER FOR YOU

The United States Bureau of Labor Statistics has a good resource known as the *Occupational Outlook Handbook,* which lists skills important in various professions. You can find it online at www.bls.gov/oco or in most public libraries and career centers. Using this resource and your results from the EQ quiz in Chapter 1, you will be able to determine whether the careers you are considering are a good fit for your skills and personality.

First, list three careers that you are interested in pursuing:

1. _____

2. _____

3. _____

Next, look up these careers in the *Occupational Outlook Handbook* to see what skills are important, paying close attention to emotional intelligence skills. (These skills are typically listed in the "Other Qualifications" section.) Look back to the EQ quiz in Chapter 1 to refresh your memory about which of the four skill areas were strengths for you.

What skills, experience, or training do you have that would fit in those careers?

_____

_____

_____

What skills or training would you still need to obtain for those careers?

_____

_____

_____

What would make it difficult for you to pursue these careers or jobs? Can you overcome these obstacles? How?

_____

_____

_____

After reviewing your weaknesses, do you think there are careers or jobs that you should avoid? Why?

_____

(continued)

(continued)

> _____
>
> _____
>
> You may want to look at other options or grow your EQ skills in your areas of weakness if you truly want to pursue a career that doesn't match your current skills.

Using Accurate Self-Assessment to Find the Right Job

Once you have done a thorough self-assessment, you will know how your skills, unique abilities, education, and experience fit with specific jobs out in the job market. You then market yourself to those particular employers and toward those targeted jobs. Research shows that people perform best and are happiest with their jobs when they are using their strengths, which are skills they are not only good at but also enjoy using. Employers also benefit from high employee satisfaction and performance.

In order to find the right position, you need to steer yourself into the right port and not just sit and wait for the wind to blow you there. You need to have a target position(s) in mind. Apply for select positions based on your knowledge of yourself, the position responsibilities, and company and industry information. It is a waste of time to do a mass mailing to as many jobs as you can find or that remotely fit what you are skilled and interested in doing. Spend your time wisely.

Clients often tell me that they want to be as open to as many jobs as possible. They feel that staying general will land them a job sooner. However, this strategy can actually work against you for a couple of reasons. First, employers are looking for more-specific expertise and will try to find the right person to fit a position. If you are too general, an employer will go with a candidate who is more targeted, trained, and looking for that particular job. Second, being open to many diverse jobs can land you in the wrong job. If you take the first job offered without considering how effective or satisfied you would be doing that job, you may later find yourself unhappy and feeling unsuccessful.

To target the right job for you, follow these tips:

- Know the skills and strengths that you want to use.

- Know the skills that employers are looking for in a candidate in that position and industry. Ask yourself whether there is a match between you and the employer.

- Talk to people in those kinds of positions through networking and setting up information meetings.

- Reflect on your values and beliefs and assess whether this job or career choice is in line with them.

- Talk to employees working in companies that are on your target list. Check out what the company values and culture are like and consider once again whether there is a fit with your values.

In addition, your resume should target the position that you are applying for. Do not make the mistake of being too broad or general on your resume. There could be hundreds of resumes received for one posted position. With such a large number of applicants for each position, hiring managers will spend less than a minute skimming your resume to see whether you have the specific skill sets and experience that they are looking for. If it appears that you do, you will be called for an interview.

Using Accurate Self-Assessment to Get the Job Offer

Knowing your strengths and weaknesses will guide you not only in selecting a career or job, but also in landing the job offer. Knowing your skills and accomplishments inside and out will help you communicate them clearly to potential employers both on a resume and in an interview.

Your resume should showcase all of your accomplishments and skills. This is why it is best to write your resume yourself. You know yourself better than anyone else, and you are the one who will be asked to elaborate on your accomplishments in an interview. Before you send your resume out to employers, it's helpful to have key people review your resume and provide basic feedback.

A good salesman knows the product that he is selling inside and out. He also has done his homework and knows the needs of his customer and how he can best meet them. He knows what strengths and skills he needs to communicate to get the customer's attention and business. In an interview, you are selling yourself and what you can contribute to the organization to make it successful. So the better you know yourself and all "your features," the better you can communicate these qualities and sell yourself to the potential employer.

Richard Bolles, in his book *What Color Is Your Parachute?,* talks about the importance of writing accomplishment stories in preparation for interviewing. In these stories, you share information about the situation, the actions that you took, and the results that were achieved for the business. You include the skill sets that you used to accomplish your results. I suggest that you go back to the exercise earlier in this chapter, "Assess Your Strengths and Weaknesses," and use your answers as a guide in writing your stories.

Lastly, use self-assessment and reflect on your appearance and presentation for an interview. You have heard how important first impressions are, and they are critical in the job search, a time when you are subjected to a high level of scrutiny. The decision on whether a candidate is potentially worth hiring is often made within minutes of the start of interview, even before the interviewer has heard answers to his questions. Therefore, it is important to be aware of the image you present, both in your dress and your mannerisms.

Check yourself; you should be able to answer yes to the following questions:

- Do you look groomed and professional?
- Do you have a firm handshake and maintain good eye contact?
- Do you smile and have a pleasant attitude?
- Do you show interest in the interviewer and his company by leaning forward and nodding your head in understanding?

By assessing yourself and communicating clearly what you have to offer through your resume, your answers to interview questions, and the way you present yourself, you will be able to make a case to an employer that you are the right person for the job.

Self-Confidence: Shining a Positive Light to Attract Employers

The third skill in self-awareness is self-confidence. *Self-confidence* means perceiving yourself in a positive way, using your strengths to achieve your goals, and being aware of your weaknesses to prevent them from getting in your way. Accomplishing one goal gives you the energy and hope to accomplish other goals.

Have you noticed that after you learn a new skill, such as how to assemble a cabinet or construct a PowerPoint presentation, you feel good about yourself and your achievement? You then feel ready to take on other challenging tasks or goals with the attitude, "I know I can do this!" When you fail, however, you lose some energy and momentum, and it often takes more effort to get back on track and to start moving forward. You have to work harder to attain your goal. Focusing on negative thoughts and feelings will make it more difficult to move ahead in your job search.

Reuven Bar-On, the developer of the EQ-i, makes a distinction in the area of self-confidence. He considers two aspects: self-regard and self-actualization. He defines *self-regard* as how good you feel about yourself. Do you hold yourself in high esteem and perceive yourself positively? Do you value yourself and all that you are? He defines *self-actualization* as how satisfied you are with yourself in relation to what you have accomplished so far in your life. Do you take part in activities that you enjoy? Are you realizing your full potential and fulfilling your goals, visions, and dreams? Both areas are equally important to think about when reflecting on your self-confidence. Self-regard focuses on the here and now, and self-actualization looks at your life in review, what you have accomplished and what you still want to achieve. If there is a large gap between these two, you might feel unfulfilled and dissatisfied with yourself and your life.

EMOTIONAL INTELLIGENCE IN ACTION

Lamont has been let go from his job position due to a downturn in business sales and profits. He has worked for 15 years as a banking manager and has a strong business and financial background. He is socially responsible and donates his time and financial skills to church organizations. In a coaching session, he shares with me that he is "not anything special" and that guys like

(continued)

(continued)

him are a dime a dozen. We explore his feelings of loss and sadness at losing his job and how this affects his self-confidence. We discuss his concerns of being more than 50 years old and back in the job market again, as well as his concerns over possible discrimination with his ethnic background.

The more we talk, the more aware he becomes of his feelings and how he is allowing his thoughts to get in the way of moving forward. He certainly cannot put a resume together selling his strengths and presenting himself as the person for the job in interviews with these kinds of negative feelings and self-defeating thoughts. With greater self-awareness and self-assessment, Lamont is able to put his thoughts into perspective and work at challenging his own negative thinking. He forces himself to be more positive in his thinking, which helps him develop a great resume that highlights his many qualifications and unique skill sets. He becomes more confident as he focuses on his diverse accomplishments and receives more interview requests in response to his resume. He admits that he feels more confidence, and he tells me that he will land a job soon.

To develop self-confidence in the job search, follow these tips:

- Thoroughly prepare for your interviews. Know and practice your answers to interview questions.

- Practice interviews with family members or friends and ask them to give you feedback on what you do well and on what you can do better.

- Accept yourself. Admit your mistakes and move on.

- Make a conscious effort not to compare yourself to others. Affirm your uniqueness. Remind yourself of your talents and strengths.

- Act confidently and visualize yourself as confident. Change the behavior, and the thoughts and emotions will follow.

- Surround yourself with positive people and positive situations. Job searching is a challenging and difficult process, and you will need the support of family, friends, and possibly a career coach.

- Focus on your strengths and accomplishments and not on your weaknesses and failures. Each day of your job search, focus on the positive and remind yourself of your accomplishments and be proud of them.

- Break challenging projects or activities in which you are lacking confidence into smaller parts and work on one part at a time. When you have accomplished one, move on to the next.

- Write down your short- and long-term goals, both in your career and personal life, and list action steps to achieve your goals. Put a timeline on each goal.

- Review your progress toward your goals on a weekly and monthly basis and make changes as needed. If you write down your weekly activities and progress, you can review your list and admire all that you have achieved this week.

Using Self-Confidence to Choose a Career

The EQ skill of self-confidence comes from having good awareness of your thoughts and feelings, knowing your strengths and weaknesses in relation to each career option, and using this information to make a good career decision. When you use your self-awareness skills to make a decision, you will be confident in the path you have chosen. Self-confidence is reassuring yourself that you are guiding yourself in the right direction.

If you are not feeling confident about your skills, education, or experience, you can work to improve that area. You can improve your skills through the exercises suggested in this book and through hands-on experience at your current job or by taking on a part-time job or doing some volunteer work. You may want to go back to school for a college degree or a certification. Remember that education can be completed on a short-term basis, such as taking a course while you are job searching, or on a long-term basis, such going to night school while working a day job to bring in the income you need while preparing yourself for the ultimate job you want.

If you are not feeling confident about your career choice, you can take a career assessment to gather information about your interests. Take a class related to the career that you are considering or volunteer in an organization or business that allows you to experience life in that profession. Both will help you to gather information to make a more informed decision, which will improve your self-confidence.

Using Self-Confidence to Find the Right Job

Persuading an employer that you are the right person for the job takes self-confidence. The role that self-confidence plays in your job search cannot be emphasized enough. If you do not have confidence that you will find a job, then you probably won't. Landing the right job is about being hopeful and optimistic, as well as being determined and motivated to do what it takes to achieve your goal.

If you are not feeling confident, you need to ask yourself why and figure out how you can get past this feeling to increase your self-confidence. For example, one theme I hear from clients is a lack of confidence in their computer skills. This lack can be remedied by developing these skills through a course at the local college or library. You have to ask yourself how important it is to improve this area to get the job you want and how motivated you are to do this.

Using Self-Confidence to Get the Job Offer

People hire people whom they like and want to be around, and people are naturally drawn to those who are self-confident. Self-confidence draws the interviewer to you, which helps create the connection that is the goal of the interview. Thus, it is more likely that you will be offered the job when you appear self-confident.

However, be careful not to come across as being arrogant. This impression can be a turn-off and place you further from your goal of connecting with the interviewer. A friend of mine who does a great deal of hiring has shared numerous stories of how people lose consideration for a job when they brag and describe themselves in grandiose terms. Who wants to work with someone who thinks he knows all the answers and is superior to everyone else in the room? Not me. Be honest with yourself and with the interviewer. Interviewing successfully is about being genuine while displaying confidence.

If you lack self-confidence, this will definitely show through in an interview. How can the interviewer be confident that you will do the job if you don't show confidence in yourself? Always act confidently in an interview even when you don't feel confident. This goes back to the thought-feelings-behavior connection. Sometimes acting as though you have the skill is the first step to learning a new skill. You start with a change in the behavior, and it leads to changes in your thoughts and feelings.

To act confidently in an interview, follow these tips:

- Make eye contact with the interviewer.

- Give a firm handshake.

- Smile.

- Stand tall and sit up straight.

- Speak with a clear, strong voice.

- Share your successes.

- Communicate solutions you provided to past problems and challenges.

- Show a can-do attitude by being enthusiastic, optimistic, and flexible in your responses.

Role Models with High Self-Awareness

As you think about your own emotional intelligence and the skills that you would like to develop further, think of people you know, both famous and in your own life, who exemplify these skills. They can serve as role models for you in working to develop your skills.

In presenting workshops on EQ, I ask the audience to think of someone who has a highly developed self-awareness. The most popular response that I receive is Oprah Winfrey. Oprah is producer and host of the award-winning *The Oprah Winfrey Show.* She is in touch with her thoughts and feelings and expresses herself well. Her emotional self-awareness enables her to relate well to others and communicate her understanding of others' perspectives. Oprah engages others while staying in touch and true to her own emotions. This genuineness allows others to trust her and feel comfortable talking with her about their life situations. She knows her strengths and weaknesses and uses this awareness to guide her in reaching her goals. She is quick to admit mistakes and takes the necessary steps to correct problems as they arise. Oprah uses her strengths, talents, and opportunities to accomplish great things for others and for our world.

Another great example of someone with a highly developed self-awareness is Katie Couric, former host of the morning show *Today* and now the first solo woman news anchor on a major television network's national evening news program. She exemplifies someone with highly developed self-awareness. She emanates genuineness, and this quality engages others and opens up more direct communication about diverse and sensitive issues. She conveys a sense of confidence in herself and shares her strengths and weaknesses openly, often using humor. She has used her self-awareness and self-confidence to take on new and risky career challenges while still maintaining her responsibilities and living her values of being a good mother, sister, and so on.

One candidate whom I worked with stands out in displaying a highly developed self-awareness. I was impressed with his self-awareness and expression of his feelings of rejection and anger after being let go from his job because of a company reorganization. He was able to share his feelings and thoughts appropriately in group discussions. He also shared how he chose to remain positive but realistic and chose to surround himself with positive people. He was open to his career assessment findings and challenged what seem to fit and what did not. He explored his interests, values, and goals and developed a job search goal and plan that he worked on daily. He was comfortable sharing his strengths with others and was forthright in sharing his weaknesses, too, sometimes slipping in a sense of humor to lighten the mood. He was optimistic that he would achieve his goals as he had in the past, and confidence emanated from him, despite being rejected for two jobs that he was interested in. After several months of searching, he landed a higher-level career position with much better pay than his previous job.

Chapter Reflections

Self-awareness is the foundation of emotional intelligence and is the first step in any successful job search. As stated in the Introduction, self-awareness is particularly important in stage I (managing emotions/self-assessment) and stage III (targeting specific jobs and careers) of the career transition process.

Three skills make up self-awareness:

- **Emotion identification** involves being aware of your feelings and linking them to the thoughts that contribute to those feelings. This awareness can help guide your response to be in line with your goals.

- **Accurate self-assessment** of your strengths and weaknesses will not only help you in choosing the right career but also will help you communicate your strengths clearly to employers on resumes and in interviews.

- **Self-confidence** means perceiving yourself in a positive way, using your strengths to achieve your goals and not letting your weaknesses get in the way.

The next step is to put self-awareness into action with self-management skills.

CHAPTER 4

Self-Management: Find Focus and Maintain Motivation

If you have self-awareness, but you do not use it to guide you, you are not putting your EQ to use. You need to develop self-management skills in addition to your self-awareness skills in order for others to see you as emotionally intelligent. Self-management is putting your self-awareness into action to affect the situation and other people.

This process involves the following four skills:

- Emotional self-control
- Adaptability
- Stress management
- Motivation

In this chapter, you will learn how to manage yourself more effectively by building these skills and applying them in your job search. The following exercise will help you determine which of these skills you most need to improve.

EQ EXERCISE: IDENTIFY AREAS OF SELF-MANAGEMENT THAT YOU NEED TO IMPROVE

Answer True or False to each of the following statements:

1. I am always hopeful. ____

2. I manage my anger in positive ways most of the time. ____

3. I adapt to new situations very well and embrace change. ____

(continued)

(continued)

4. I view myself as a positive person. ____

5. I am patient most of the time. ____

6. I can make minor adjustments without feeling overwhelmed. ____

7. I enjoy the people whom I work with. ____

8. When stressful situations arise, I seem to manage them better than my coworkers. ____

9. I like solving problems, and I am very skilled at it. ____

10. I keep striving toward my goal even when things get difficult. ____

11. Sometimes I get anxious, but it does not affect my work. ____

12. When I start something new, I am confident that I will do well. ____

13. I enjoy my job and look forward to going to work. ____

14. Even when I get frustrated, I remain calm. ____

15. I manage change easily and seem to adapt better than others. ____

16. I am confident in my ability to deal with tough situations. ____

17. I can control my anger and frustration effectively. ____

18. I like to stop and think before making a decision. ____

19. I handle stress without getting too frazzled. ____

20. I like to try new things. ____

Scoring

To score your answers, count the number of statements that you marked False in each set and write that number on the corresponding line.

Set 1: Emotional Self-Control/Stress Management

Look at numbers 2, 5, 8, 11, 14, 17, and 19. How many of these statements were false? _____

Set 2: Adaptability

Look at numbers 3, 6, 9, 12, 15, 18, and 20. How many of these statements were false? _____

Set 3: Motivation/Optimism

Look at numbers 1, 4, 7, 10, 13, and 16. How many of these statements were false? _____

Any set in which you answered False to three or more items is likely an area in which you need to grow your self-management skills for a more productive job search.

Emotional Self-Control

Emotional self-control is the ability to manage emotions in a positive and effective way. It starts with an awareness of a feeling and is followed by a process of actively managing how the feeling is expressed. Gaining control of your feelings involves reflecting on the thoughts that are creating the feelings. Reflecting on positive feelings such as happiness or excitement and expressing these feelings is easy because they are pleasant to experience. They are usually welcomed by those around you. It is much more difficult to reflect on and experience frustration and anger. These feelings are uncomfortable to feel and express. They are often seen as negative, and their expression is often discouraged by others due to the discomfort it causes. Yet both positive and negative feelings serve a purpose and give you information to help you figure out what is going on and how to respond.

EQ EXERCISE: PREPARE STRATEGIES TO DEAL WITH INTENSE NEGATIVE EMOTIONS

During the job search process, you may feel strong emotions such as anger, rejection, and sadness. Emotional self-control involves being able to develop strategies to handle these emotions. When you start feeling bad during the job search, answer these questions:

1. What are you feeling? For example, do you feel angry? Rejected? Sad? _____

(continued)

(continued)

2. What negative thoughts are contributing to that feeling? Here are some examples:

"Nobody is responding to my phone calls and e-mail messages to tell me whether I got the job I interviewed for. That's not a good sign."

"I didn't do as well as I thought at the interview, because I just got a rejection letter."

"I don't have the education I need to get the job I want, nor do I have the time or money to get the education now."

_____

_____

3. What self-talk can you use to challenge and change those negative thoughts to more-realistic and -positive ones? For example, the following statements provide positive and realistic responses to the examples of negative thoughts in question 2:

"Although the result of my interview is important to me, it may not be a priority to others. I will choose to stay hopeful until I hear otherwise."

"It hurts to be rejected, but it is not a reflection on me as a person or as a professional. I have many great assets and much to offer the right company."

"I am in a tough situation. I most likely will have to take a less desirable job now to pay for the training I need for my dream job. I know that eventually I'll reach my goal."

_____

_____

4. What action can you take to move on and affect your feelings in a positive way? Here are some examples:

Stop thinking and complaining about getting no response from that particular company and focus on other job opportunities.

Push the rejection from your mind and continue working to find the right opportunity.

Find a job that you are qualified for now. Once you are earning an income, you can enroll in courses to achieve the education you need to obtain that dream job.

_____

_____

Sometimes you may not be ready to work on changing a thought, so the best way to manage it is to put it out of your mind temporarily. You make a conscious choice that as that thought comes to your mind, you push it out again. You tell yourself that you are not going to deal with it now. You may then choose to engage in other activities to get your mind off that thought. By doing this, you can help yourself feel less stressed and move on to the task at hand.

For example, say you have a conflict with your teenage son before you leave for work one morning. You have many upsetting thoughts and feelings as you drive to work, but when you arrive at your job, you need to focus on your work responsibilities. You decide not to think about the conflict with your son until you return home; you force yourself to focus your thoughts and energies on your work. In this way, you are controlling your thoughts and managing feelings to better deal with the situation.

EMOTIONAL INTELLIGENCE IN ACTION

Van is aware that he is extremely nervous for an upcoming interview. He has been practicing answers to questions over and over again, and he feels tension in his head and a sick feeling in his stomach when he thinks about the interview.

(continued)

(continued)

His self-talk entails statements such as, "I need this job. I have been without a job for a year now. I have been on 10 job interviews, and no one wants to hire me. I am a failure." How will Van do in this upcoming interview? Probably poorly if he continues to dwell on this negative thinking.

Van is aware of his emotions; now he has to manage them so that he can perform effectively in the interview. How can he do this? First, he changes his negative self-talk statements into positive ones, such as, "I am interested in this job, and I am looking forward to the interview to learn more about it. I know I have many skills and strengths that would enable me to be successful in this position, and I would be an asset to this company." He focuses on thinking only positive thoughts and getting rid of all negative ones. He then takes action to manage his anxiety by limiting the time he practices his answers to just once in the morning. The day before the interview, he also drives to the interview site so that he is familiar with the directions and travel time. He arrives early on the day of the interview and takes several deep breaths to lessen his anxiety. During the interview, Van comes across as less anxious and more confident.

Another aspect of managing your emotions is being able to delay gratification of your impulses and needs in service of longer-term goals. For example, your friends might want you to go to a ball game with them the night before you have an important interview. You would like to go to the ball game and enjoy yourself, but you know that you also need to finish up some research on the company and get plenty of rest because the interview is at 8 in the morning. You need to get a job, so doing well in this interview is important. So you put off your desire for fun in service of the higher goal and decline the offer to attend the ball game. You manage your immediate impulses and needs by reflecting on what is important and what you need to do to act in service of your goal and respond in a way that moves you closer to that goal.

Adaptability

Change is a part of life. There are big changes, such as ending one job and beginning another, and small changes, such as canceling an appointment and rescheduling it for another day. Because we are creatures of habit, change is also a stressor. Changing our routines and ways of doing things can be difficult and requires more thought and effort than it would to do things in the same way. Yet embracing change and being flexible can bring new opportunities and creative solutions. This self-management skill is called *adaptability*.

Embracing change by expecting it and being ready for it will give you a more positive and proactive mindset to deal with it. Allow yourself some time to think and talk about your situation and problems, but then move yourself forward. Staying focused on the negatives will likely make matters worse. Feeling anxious and stressed will take away some of the energy that you need to direct toward resolving problems and accomplishing the work at hand.

Adaptability is about looking at all the options. For example, what happens if you have always taken the same road to work and one day you find that the road is closed and under construction? You have to find a different route. If you have never ventured a different route, you will have to learn a new route immediately. What if the new route saves you 10 minutes in getting to work? Wow. The usual route is not the most effective one. And you might never have learned about the new, quicker route if not for the construction change. Being open to new ways and trying new things presents more possibilities. The more possibilities you consider, the greater your chances of choosing an optimum solution. You have more information or knowledge, which can lead to more power.

As you can see, the skill of adaptability encompasses the ability to be an effective problem solver. According to most researchers, thorough problem solving is basically a seven-step process:

1. Identify the problem.
2. Assess and evaluate the problem.
3. Generate possible solutions.
4. Analyze each of the possible solutions.
5. Select the best one.
6. Make a plan and take action.
7. Evaluate the outcome.

When you solve problems, you become conscious of your thinking process and focused on the goal of resolving the problem.

In the book *The EQ Edge: Emotional Intelligence and Your Success,* authors Steven Stein and Howard Book write about two capacities that are at play when you are a successful problem solver. Both are facets of emotional intelligence at work. The first is *intuition* or using your hunches and impressions. Using hunches and impressions as early warning signals can help to identify possible problems. If you are able to pick up on cues that a problem is brewing and then examine them rather than dismiss or overlook them, you have a head start when and if the problem materializes. Intuition goes back to self-awareness, in which the better in touch you can be with your thoughts and feelings, the more you can use them to guide your decisions and actions. The less aware of these cues you are, the more you lose out on pertinent information, which can leave you open for making the wrong choices or decisions and then experiencing dissatisfaction and failure.

The second capacity at play in problem solving is *innovation*, which is the capacity to come up with new ways of viewing the situation and deriving possible solutions. This skill is also about using your creativity and being open to exploring novel ideas and unknown territory. Innovation must also take into account an accurate sense of reality, because potential risks are involved. When innovation is tempered with this awareness and management, good results can follow.

When you become aware that you are being too set in your ways, challenge yourself to be more flexible. Start with self-awareness and move to self-management. Working on adaptability in other areas of your life will help you develop this trait in your job search. For example, take a household chore that you do often. You have probably done it the same way for many years. Now think of another way to do the chore. Try it and see if it works better.

EMOTIONAL INTELLIGENCE IN ACTION

Rosemary has always wanted to be a teacher, which requires at least a four-year degree. She lives in a rural area and can only afford to commute to the local community college, which offers only an associate degree. The university that offers the four-year degree is 300 miles away and is expensive. Some people might look at these circumstances and give up on the dream of being a teacher and settle for an unsatisfying occupation, but not Rosemary. She adapts and finds a way to work toward her long-term goal. After much thought, Rosemary decides to get a job at the local factory where she could work second shift and attend the community college during the day. In this way, she can earn a two-year degree and make enough money to apply to and attend the university to finish her education and achieve her goal of a degree in teaching. She has to work very hard, but she is motivated to do what she needs to do to be successful.

EQ EXERCISE: IMPROVE YOUR ADAPTABILITY SKILLS FOR THE JOB SEARCH

When you are looking for a job, it's a good idea to give yourself some structure. For example, if you are unemployed, you might plan to work from 8 a.m. to 5 p.m. each weekday on your job search as if it were your job. However, you don't want to get stuck in an unproductive rut. Use you adaptability to open yourself up to new ways of finding a job.

Look at your current job search routine. Is it working for you or do you need to make some changes to it? For example, do you need to exercise midway through the day to vary your activities, or do you need to schedule networking meetings at lunchtime so you can get out of the house?

Look at how you are approaching the job market. How much time do you spend looking online for job postings, setting up and attending networking meetings, researching companies, and so on? Do you need to make changes to your strategy? What is working and what is not? How can you change it and when will you start?

Talk to mentors, friends, and family members about your job search strategy and ask them for their thoughts as they listen to you talk about your job search efforts. Can they suggest any other ways to approach the job market? Can they make any suggestions on how you can be more effective? Are you willing to try their ideas and see if they work? Pushing yourself to try new things increases your flexibility.

Finally, reflect on your problem-solving approach. Take a recent problem and ask yourself whether you followed the seven-step process. Did you miss any steps? If so, how did it affect the solution? Plan to focus on that step the next time a problem arises.

Combining Emotional Self-Control and Adaptability for an Effective Job Search

Events such as losing a job or graduating and looking for a job for the first time provoke many feelings. For example, feelings of anger and/or sadness are a common reaction to losing a job. When looking for a job for the first time, you might feel a lot of anxiety, frustration, and uncertainty because the job search process is new to you. Be aware of your feelings and manage them by dealing with them positively and by challenging unrealistic or negative thoughts. Not managing your feelings in the job search will make you less effective. Feelings can interfere with your having positive interactions while networking or being interviewed. Emotional self-control is critical to keeping focused for an effective job search.

Controlling emotions involves adaptability. The goal is to assess the emotions, deal with them effectively, and move on in service of your ultimate goal. You have to maneuver through diverse and challenging tasks involved in a job search, and doing so takes openness to learning and resilience. In the following sections, I explain how you can use emotional self-control and adaptability together to choose a career, find the right job, and get the job offer.

Using Emotional Self-Control and Adaptability to Choose a Career

Once you are aware of your skills and interests, you can develop a plan on how to explore that career choice. It takes emotional self-control to map out and stick to a plan. You may need to use self-talk to remind yourself not to stray from your plan or direction based on a whim. You want to be flexible and evaluate new information as you explore your interests but then decide in a thoughtful and conscious way if you need to make changes in your plan.

For example, say that you want to work in a government position, such as for the United States Post Office. Upon talking to postal workers and doing some research, you learn how this industry continues to decline due to the Internet and related technology. You have to think through whether you still want to go in this direction or whether you need to consider a plan B. Considering other career options at this point would be a sign of adaptability. Considering other options also takes emotional self-control and discipline because you have to step back from the direction that you were going, reflect, and take steps in another direction.

Certain occupations require significant education and training. Obtaining this education and training requires emotional self-control, because you have to delay gratification of your needs. For example, people who become doctors are above average in their ability to delay gratification. They have to spend large amounts of money for many years of schooling, which means they have to go without some material possessions in pursuit of their goal. They also have to spend a great deal of time and exert much mental effort and physical endurance to pass academic courses and complete internships and residencies. The demands of preparing for this profession mean more time studying and less time playing—all for the long-term goal of being a doctor. When considering careers, you need to assess how much self-control you have and how long you can delay gratification. If this is an area of weakness, it might be more realistic to consider a two-year college, possibly one that has a cooperative program in which you can work while going to school.

Using Emotional Self-Control and Adaptability to Find the Right Job

To be successful in getting the job you want, you will have to draw on many of your self-management skills. For example, it takes self-control to not be in a hurry to get your resume out the door. I believe it is more important to spend time doing a quality resume first, and then send it out so that it will be an effective and targeted document.

Making your resume great entails describing your accomplishments in ways that will grab an employer's attention. You must whittle your great accomplishment stories to single statements that highlight the results you have achieved in your past positions. This telling of your past successes is meant to show your potential for future success.

Great resume writing takes effort. You will have to write and rewrite your resume, edit it a number of times, and edit it again after asking a couple of trusted people to review and critique it. You might become frustrated or impatient, but don't let these emotions push you off your path. Use your emotional self-control skills to manage your emotions and direct your energies to keep working on that resume.

Suppose you receive a rejection letter or phone call for a job you really wanted. You feel weighed down with sadness, anger, rejection, insecurity, and self-doubt. These feelings are natural; any rejection can shake your confidence. Although you should acknowledge these feelings, don't dwell on them. Doing so will interfere with your success.

Instead, you need to adapt and change your thoughts and behavior. Clients sometimes ask, "How do I get my confidence back?" I suggest focusing on your past accomplishments and what you can do or have influence over as the best approach. You might choose to focus on thoughts such as, "I am not going to let this job rejection get me down. I have too much to offer. My skills and experience have gotten me in the door before, and they will again. I will find the right job, hopefully sooner rather than later. I will keep working and trying." This type of positive self-talk will bring feelings of hope, optimism, renewed energy, and enthusiasm in pursuit of your goal.

You need to add realistic thinking and problem solving, too. You might need to step back and reassess whether you have the skills and experience needed for the position that you are targeting. If the answer is yes, keep doing what you are doing; the job is out there, and you will find it and land it.

Using Emotional Self-Control and Adaptability to Get the Job Offer

Controlling your emotions and adapting to the situation at hand are critical in an interview. Research shows that much of what people believe about others comes from observation and interpretation of nonverbal cues. So when you are networking with business contacts or interviewing with potential employers, it is important to remember that what you do is equally important as what you say. Information is gathered from two different perspectives: content and process. *Content* is what a person says; *process* is how the person says it, meaning what was implied, left out, or not said directly but communicated in a nonverbal way such as through facial expressions, body posture, tone of voice, and touch, such as the handshake. Observing the process of communication is being in tune with information and data that you take in that is derived from your senses: what you see, smell, taste, touch, and hear.

Remember that employers are looking for people who are emotionally intelligent. The following list explains some ways that you can show employers that you are adaptable and manage your emotions well:

- Take some notes during the interview. Later that day, thank the interviewer in an e-mail message that references some of the things that you discussed. Following up in this way shows that you are self-disciplined.

- Demonstrate patience by allowing the person interviewing you to do more of the leading, talking, and directing. Do not interrupt her or try to dominate the discussion. If you are feeling impatient, ask yourself what is making you feel impatient. Is it because the interviewer hasn't given you information that you need to know? If so, take action by asking the question again, maybe in a different way. Is it because the interviewer is talking a lot and you haven't had the opportunity to share pertinent information? Then take action and speak up at the first opportunity to let the interviewer know any important information that you want to share about your skills, expertise, and experience before the interview is over.

- To show adaptability, change your posture to match the interviewer. If he is relaxed, you can relax (but don't slouch). If he is leaning forward, you should also lean forward, perched in your chair. This change shows in a subtle way that you are following his lead and adapting to the situation.

- If you make a mistake in the interview, rebound from it quickly. Do not dwell on it, and do not give up. Show your resilience by continuing to do your very best to convince the interviewer that you are the person for the job.

Stress Management

An important part of self-management is stress management. *Stress management* is your ability to deal with stress without falling apart and becoming too frazzled. It is using positive coping strategies to deal effectively with a situation. Dealing with stress effectively definitely helps you in a job search.

Being out of a job and not knowing how and when you will find another one is a huge stressor for many reasons. First, there are the immediate concerns of paying the rent and bills. Second is the uncertainty of how long this unemployment is going to last. The lack of routine also is difficult for some to manage because humans are creatures of routine and habit. When you are unemployed, you have more time on your hands to think and be worried, which can make the situation feel worse. Lastly, you are likely to have to deal with feelings of rejection as a result of the job search process.

The better able you are to deal with stress, the more effective you will be in controlling your feelings of anger, frustration, and impatience. These things go hand in hand. Have you noticed that, when you are under extreme stress, you become angrier quicker and more impatient? Your system cannot function as effectively because you are feeling overwhelmed and your brain is in overdrive mode. Think of a car. The faster you drive, the less control you have and the more difficult it is to maneuver the turns and to stop. Your job is to monitor yourself and put on the brakes. By slowing down, you will have more control over your thoughts and thus your feelings and your actions.

The goal is to manage your emotions rather than be controlled by them. Self-management is being aware of your feelings and taking action. The action could be pausing, assessing, venting, or planning the next action to take to maximize your benefits from the situation. You are tuning in to the stress that you are experiencing and managing it through changing your thoughts and behaviors to ones that place you in line with your goal and thus can relieve the emotion and stress that you are experiencing.

EMOTIONAL INTELLIGENCE IN ACTION

For 20 years, Yesenia has worked as a shipping and receiving clerk for a distribution center. Now that the company she works for is closing this center, she is being forced into the job market. She doesn't know how to go about finding a job, but she knows she needs to find one quickly because she is a single parent with three children to support. Recognizing that she feels overwhelmed and extremely anxious, she calls family and friends for support and help. She asks her sister to watch her children while she goes on interviews, thereby cutting the cost of the after-school program. She talks with her brother-in-law, who is knowledgeable about job searching, and asks him for guidance in writing a resume and networking. To improve her nonexistent computer skills, she enrolls in a computer training course at the local library and gets a free e-mail address to use for her job search.

The more Yesenia continues to take action steps, the more positive energy she creates and is able to use during those times when obstacles get in her way. She chooses not to let the stress overwhelm her and continues to take action after assessing her emotions and the realities of her situation each step of the way. She eventually finds a position in a smaller company closer to her house, which allows her to have more time with her children. She also has a chance to practice her newly acquired computer skills!

EQ EXERCISE: MANAGE STRESS IN YOUR JOB SEARCH

To manage stress both during your job search and throughout the rest of your life, take care of your physical self:

- **Exercise regularly.** Exercise releases endorphins, which are chemicals in the body that fight off the physiological effects of stress on your body. Exercise also helps you to feel better because you are taking proactive steps to be in charge of your body and physical state. In addition, sometimes you can come up with creative ideas when you exercise. Experts recommend workouts of at least 30 minutes three times a week.

- **Relax.** Working all the time drains your body and your mind. Taking a break and allowing yourself to relax and focus on other less-intense topics allows your body and mind to recover and reenergize. When you go back to work after a weekend of relaxation, you are ready to work and better able to effectively manage the stressors that arise. Find a hobby that will allow you to relax your mind and body and use some of your other skills and talents. You may even feel a sense of pride and confidence from your accomplishment that will carry over to your job search.

- **Sleep.** Getting the right amount of sleep can't be emphasized enough. When you are tired, your mind and body move slower and do not function as well. Concerns and worries grow out of perspective because you are not using all of your controls and not putting them into place as quickly. When you are tired, refrain from putting too much thought and action into worries and concerns. Let things go until the morning when you are feeling refreshed.

- **Breathe deeply.** Take a few deep breaths, allowing your lungs to fill completely with air and then slowly exhaling. This action calms your physiological and emotional state and is a good tool to use whenever you need to pause and quickly assess the situation to make an effective response. It is especially useful during interviews when you are likely to feel anxious.

Motivation

Motivation is a force or influence that moves you to act and is the driver of your job search. It pushes you to establish goals and then direct your energy toward attaining them.

To tap into the power of motivation, you first need to understand what motivates you. Your motivations can and do change over time and are related to your needs. Psychologist Abraham Maslow stated that we continue to strive to meet a hierarchy of needs to develop our full potential as a human being. If we become blocked in this process, we become unhappy and dissatisfied. This hierarchy of needs starts with the basic physical needs of food and water and progresses to safety needs. Social needs for belonging and love are the next level, followed by esteem needs such as self-respect and recognition from others. The last and highest need is self-actualization, which is being the best that you can possibly be.

Your values will also drive your motivation. As you learned in Chapter 3, identifying your values can guide you to make decisions that support your values and thus lead to life and job satisfaction.

Motivation comes from not only your needs and values but also from your goals. An old saying states, "If you don't know where you are going, you might not get there." A clear awareness of your goals will guide you to take the needed actions to achieve them. Thinking about the goal and how it will meet your needs, values, and interests if you achieve it can bring desire and energy to propel you in that direction. If you do not have a goal, you lack energy and a driving force.

EQ EXERCISE: COMPILE RECORDS OF YOUR JOB SEARCH

Collecting all the information pertaining to your job transition in a folder on your computer or in a binder can help you be organized and stay focused on your goals. Here are some items you might want to include:

- Summary of skills, accomplishments, interests, and values.

- List of potential jobs and industries that you want to explore.

- Research on jobs and industries.

- Contact information for people whom you want to connect with to gather information. Keep track of when you meet with someone and the information you learn as a result of your meeting. Note whether you want to stay in contact with that person through e-mail, phone, or another meeting. Also, set a schedule for how often you should contact people, such as once a month.

- Records of interview dates, information learned from the interview, unanswered questions or missing information, and dates to follow up regarding outcome of the interview with that organization.

- List of what is important to you in a job and career. You can look at this information when you have a job offer or are deciding between multiple offers. Use this information to help you make an informed decision about whether this is the right job for you.

- Your job offer letter and job acceptance letter.

- Your resume, cover letters, and any other important information you might want to keep as aids for future job searches.

Optimism goes hand in hand with motivation. Optimism keeps you going through the rough spots and obstacles that get in the way as you strive toward your goals. Optimism is a focus on positive thinking that, like all of the other emotional intelligence skills, can be learned. According to psychologist Martin Seligman in his book *Learned Optimism: How to Change Your Mind and Your Life,* many studies show data that indicate that optimistic people are generally healthier and live longer.

Optimism starts with an awareness of the negative thoughts that you play in your mind and moves you to challenge those negative thoughts and change them to more realistic and positive ones. Being a pessimist by choosing to focus on the negative side of a matter can keep you feeling stuck, powerless, and hopeless. With positive thoughts, you can keep moving forward.

Optimism in the job search can be choosing to look at and focus on the benefits and opportunities you have as a result of losing your job. For example, some of my clients have told me they were able to complete projects around the house or start an exercise program with the time they had away from work. Others have shared that they likely would not have left their job if it weren't for this push out the door. They were actually glad to have this opportunity.

I learned the powerful lesson of the benefits of having a positive attitude from my dad. He began working at age 12 and paid his way through college. He graduated with a degree in engineering and began as a foreman in a large steel-producing company. Through hard work and his sense of commitment over a 30-year period, he was promoted to supervisor, plant director, and then a corporate position. One of his biggest accomplishments came when he was a plant director. Working with a limited budget and resources, he successfully lead his teams to turn an outdated, high-cost steel mill into one of the company's largest steel-producing plants. Many were skeptical, and he had some realistic concerns, but he believed it could be done and kept a positive attitude, despite obstacles and adversity. He refrained from negative thinking and saw problems as challenges. His positive attitude and confidence spread to those who worked with him, and they were able to accomplish great results as a team. With a positive attitude, I also have accomplished the goals that I have set out to achieve in my life, and I believe others can do the same.

Some people have more challenges and crises to face than others, but everyone experiences setbacks and problems. Although you have no control over these events in and of themselves, you can control your response to them. You can look at any event and ask what you have learned from it and how you can move forward. In this way, you gain wisdom and become stronger in your resolve to achieve your goals. If you are optimistic and motivated, every failure can be another step on the path to success!

EMOTIONAL INTELLIGENCE IN ACTION

John is a junior at the local college, where he has changed his major three times and struggles with grades. He also works at the local grocery store where his sister also worked, but he doesn't like it much. He used to like to draw, but he gave that up after high school graduation when he was not accepted into art school. He doubts whether he will be able to find anything he likes to do. With this pessimistic attitude, he is not motivated to take steps toward checking into other programs or colleges and does not try to network with others.

A family friend who works in a construction company tells him about a summer opening at the company that pays more than his grocery store job. John applies and is hired. He finds that he enjoys waking up at an early hour to go to work everyday, and he likes working with his hands and as part of a team to build something. He feels relieved that he does not have to study for a class. After several weeks on the job, he realizes that he does not value further college education. He instead values creativity, productivity, and adventure, and he needs these qualities in his job to stay motivated and happy. He chooses to drop out of the four-year college and attend a vocational school to study environmental technology while working full-time at the job that he loves.

EQ EXERCISE: SET GOALS TO MOTIVATE YOURSELF

Clarify your goals. Write out your long-term and short-term career goals. For each goal, write ways you will achieve this goal. For example, what actions will you take? Establish a timeline for each goal as well. Finally, consider what possible obstacles you might encounter and how you will deal with them.

Long-Term Goals

Goal: _____

Ways to achieve goal:_____

_____

Timeline: _____

Obstacles: _____

_____

Ways to deal with obstacles: _____

_____

Goal: _____

Ways to achieve goal:_____

_____

Timeline: _____

Obstacles: _____

_____

Ways to deal with obstacles: _____

_____

(continued)

(continued)

Short-Term Goals

Goal: _____

Ways to achieve goal:_____

_____

Timeline: _____

Obstacles: _____

_____

Ways to deal with obstacles: _____

_____

Goal: _____

Ways to achieve goal:_____

_____

Timeline: _____

Obstacles: _____

_____

Ways to deal with obstacles: _____

_____

Combining Stress Management, Motivation, and Optimism for a Powerful Job Search

Managing stress is accomplished through managing the emotions that arise in response to stressors in life. Managing emotions goes back to changing thoughts and behaviors with the end result in mind. Changing thoughts to be more realistic and positive is acting with optimism and choosing to see the bright side of the situation. Changing behaviors to be in line with your desired outcome or goal puts you in motion and further motivates you to keep moving in that direction. In the pages ahead I share how stress management, motivation, and optimism combine and can be used in choosing a career, finding the right job, and getting the job offer.

Using Stress Management and Motivation to Choose a Career

Choosing a satisfying career can be difficult and can involve a lot of work. You need to assess your interests, skills, and personality; research your options; and then acquire the necessary training and education. To accomplish all this, you need motivation.

Remember that motivation comes from needs, values, and goals. Matching your values and needs with a career that supports them will help you make a good choice. To find this career, you will need to set some goals for yourself. For example, you might set the goal of getting some experience with a career you are considering to see whether you will like it. To achieve this goal, you can volunteer or get a part-time job in the field or career that you are considering. This experience will provide more information to you about the environment, job, industry, and kinds of people in this career. Doing this extra work on top of school and other responsibilities requires energy and drive.

EQ EXERCISE: FIND A MOTIVATING CAREER

List your needs. What do you need out of your job/career?

_____

_____

Go back and look at your top five values from the exercise in Chapter 3. Write down your top five values below.

1. _____

2. _____

3. _____

(continued)

(continued)

4. _____

5. _____

Which jobs appeal to you at this time?

_____

_____

Which of these jobs or careers are in line with your values?

_____

_____

If you are skilled at managing stress, you might want to consider a job in which you can use this skill. Some jobs require individuals with a high *stress tolerance,* meaning that it takes a lot of stressors before they become overwhelmed. For example, lawyers deal with conflict and stressful situations in their work and need high stress tolerance and good stress management skills in order to be effective. If stress management is not an area of strength, you might want to stay away from higher-stress jobs.

A good resource to use to find out this sort of information about careers is the O*NET database, which is compiled by the U.S. Department of Labor. You can search through this information by going online to http://online.onetcenter.org. The job descriptions include measures such as stress tolerance and specific stressful situations (for example, dealing with unpleasant or angry people or conflict situations).

Using Stress Management and Motivation to Find the Right Job

Job searching isn't for the weak-minded; it requires determination and persistence. Determination keeps your goal always in sight and helps you overcome obstacles to reach it. Persistence makes it possible to stick to the immediate task despite the many feelings that arise to challenge you. For example, working around schedules to set up networking meetings and interviews takes adaptability and persistence. When you try to schedule a meeting, there may be some phone tag or large gaps in response time. Be persistent and don't give up. Monitor your feelings and think positively.

In order to find the right job to apply to, you have to believe there is a job out there that you want and can do, and that you will interview well enough to get the job offer. Having these beliefs then helps you to feel self-assured and act confidently. When you exude confidence, others see you as optimistic.

If you doubt yourself and your ability, negative thoughts abound, which lead to negative feelings and stress. Managing stress well helps you to be clear about the situation and respond effectively.

When you achieve your goals, you become confident that you can achieve other goals that you set for yourself. This confidence comes from having faith in yourself and believing you can create influence. Of course, you might not be successful at first, but you can choose to view failures as obstacles or use them as motivators. The idea is that if you continue to try and make changes to your efforts, eventually you will succeed.

When you face obstacles, you must reassess the situation and ask yourself some questions:

- Have you set realistic goals?
- Have you done all in your power and control to achieve the goal? Are you truly motivated to achieve your goal?
- Do you really want to achieve this goal, and, if so, are you ready for what comes with your success?

This type of self-talk helps you to reflect back on your thoughts, feelings, and behaviors and use them as a guide.

When you are searching for the right job, be aware of your motivation as you explore the job responsibilities. When you are motivated, you are energetic and involved in directing your energy in pursuit of a goal, and others experience your enthusiasm. Do you feel energy and enthusiasm as you think or talk about the job? Do you feel confident that you can be successful in the tasks involved? Reflecting on your experience can help you decide whether it is the right job for you.

Using Stress Management and Motivation to Get the Job Offer

Remember the saying "What you see is what you get"? I believe this is true in the interview. The interviewer can get a glimpse of how you deal with stress and how motivated you are to do the job by the content of your answers and the way in which you present yourself and your responses. I have had job candidates tell me that some interviewers purposefully say things to provoke a response in order to test stress management.

Even when interviewers aren't testing you, the interviewing process can be stressful. When you are called to interview all day at a company with one interview scheduled after another followed by dinner in the evening, you need to show endurance and good self-management. You are on the spot and under inspection all day, which can be emotionally and physically draining. You want to perform well and rise to the challenge.

To perform well in the interview, you have to manage your anxiety. If you let your anxiety and worry overwhelm you, you risk not communicating information pertinent to your ability to handle the job. Being anxious makes convincing the interviewer that you have confidence in yourself and in your abilities even more difficult. The interviewer's response to your anxiety may be doubt about whether you can do the job, especially if a high degree of stress management skill is needed.

Not only do you need to manage your stress, but also you need to communicate your motivation and optimism. Think of the kind of people whom you like to be around. Are you drawn to lifeless, lazy, slow-moving, pessimistic people? Probably not. Neither is the interviewer.

During the interview, you can demonstrate your motivation and ability to manage stress in specific ways:

- Politely re-ask a question that was left unanswered by the interviewer to show persistence.

- Demonstrate energy by raising your voice tone and using animated facial expressions.

- Lean forward instead of slouching back in your chair to show that you are ready to work and eager to listen.

- Respond to questions in a positive way that shows you can handle the situation and that you are optimistic and confident that a solution can be reached.

- Smile and show a sense of humor. Smiling can be a very engaging action, and laughing with the interviewer is sharing something in common. Smiling and laughing can bond people and enhance the connection and communication. Using humor and a smile also reduces tension and stress that you may feel in an interview.

Role Models with High Self-Management

When I give seminars and ask for examples of individuals with high self-management skills, I always get examples of individuals who lack self-management skills. Identifying people who have let their emotions get out of control is easy, often because their behavior has led to serious or dangerous consequences. However, there are some people who I think demonstrate high levels of self-management skills.

One person with high emotional self-control and stress management skills is Rudolph Giuliani, who was mayor of New York City during the time of the September 11 attacks on the World Trade Center. He exemplifies an emotionally intelligent leader in that he was highly aware of both his and others' emotions and used that knowledge to manage his and others' emotions and to guide his actions. In this very stressful situation, he maintained his composure and visited emergency teams, providing support and guidance to them. He answered questions and addressed community concerns while letting others know he was experiencing the same emotions of shock and grief as they were. He conveyed his firm commitment and optimism that New York City and the United States of America would get through this crisis by working together.

Another individual with high self-management skills is Bill Gates, who seems to be very adaptable and motivated in running his successful business and in contributing to his community. Bill dropped out of Harvard University to follow his passion. He started his own business, which lead to the era of personal computers. He has continued to adapt to changing markets and keep his company in the forefront, becoming one of the wealthiest men in the world.

One of my clients, who was let go from his company during a reorganization, impressed me with his high self-management skills. He was in his sixties and facing a difficult job market, but he was confident that he would find a company interested in his expertise in quality control. He was adaptable and allowed himself to be open to new ideas from me, from the outplacement program services in which he was enrolled, and from others whom he networked with through this career transition. He was passionate about what he did, and it showed. He managed his emotions well and shared his thoughts and feelings with others, which encouraged them to do the same. He certainly did not let the stress of his situation overwhelm him, although he identified it was there. He stayed enthusiastic and positive throughout the process. Within a few months of leaving his prior position, he received an offer from a midsize company that hired him for a five-year contract to lead the company's directive to improve and expand quality control processes in the United States and abroad.

Chapter Reflections

As you might remember from the Introduction, self-management plays a key part in stage IV (interviewing for positions) of the career transition process. Self-management is putting your self-awareness into action to change the situation and influence others in the service of achieving your goals in the moment or over a period of time.

The job search will evoke many feelings, and using your awareness and understanding of them will give you important information to aid you. The ability to manage your emotions in a positive and effective way is called emotional self-control and is a key self-management skill.

The self-management skill of adaptability encompasses your ability to be an effective problem solver, in which you brainstorm and evaluate many possible solutions and choose and implement the best one. Embracing change and being adaptable can bring new opportunities and creative solutions to your job search.

Stress management also will move you ahead in your job search. The better you can deal with stress, the more effective you will be in controlling your feelings of anger, frustration, and impatience.

Knowing what motivates you and staying in line with that motivation keeps you on the right track to choosing a career or finding a job that satisfies you. Optimism works with motivation to move you toward your goals.

Now that you have a good understanding of the personal competencies of self-awareness and self-management, it is time to focus on the social competencies: social awareness and social skills.

CHAPTER 5

Social Awareness: Empathize with Employers and Make the Most of Opportunities

What happens when you are so focused on yourself that you are totally clueless as to what is going on around you? Sometimes when I am presenting a workshop, one individual dominates the question-and-answer session. He asks a lot of questions, and often they are only pertinent to his particular situation. Others in the group become frustrated with this person because he seems so focused on himself and lacks regard for those around him. They are therefore less likely to connect, network, or reach out to help him. If he were more socially aware, he would limit his questions to those that relate to and can help everyone in the group at the time. He could then ask me the specific questions privately after the workshop.

When you live in a world with people, you are ultimately affected by them. When you ignore them or their influence, you act with less knowledge and are likely to be less effective. Just as you need to have self-awareness in order to manage yourself, you need social awareness in order to manage others. Social awareness is composed of three skills or competencies:

- Empathy
- Reality testing
- Social responsibility

As you learned in Chapter 2, your personal skills and social skills are interconnected. They build on one another and can offset one another. So the more developed your self-awareness and self-management skills are, the better skilled you can be at social awareness. This chapter explains how you can add social awareness skills to what you have already learned to make the connections that will help your career.

The Feedback Loop

As you might remember from the discussion of the EQ Connection Triangle in Chapter 2, self-awareness and self-management entail working with your own connections to guide your behavior effectively. Social awareness and social skills involve not only using your own connections but also being aware of and managing others' feelings, behaviors, and thoughts when they express them. This connection between people is called the *feedback loop,* and Figure 5.1 shows how it works.

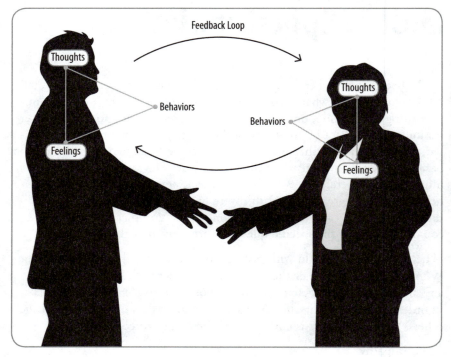

Figure 5.1. The feedback loop.

The social awareness skill of empathy is a pivotal part of the feedback loop. Empathy is the ability to read another person's emotions and behavior and understand that person's perspective. Being able to complete the loop by responding appropriately is a sign of emotional intelligence.

Related to empathy is the ability to read situations accurately, which is known as reality testing. This skill involves monitoring and challenging your thoughts (and possibly changing them if they are not realistic) in response to your environment and what the other people around you say and do.

When multiple people are involved, the skill of social responsibility comes into play. Social responsibility is your ability to consider the needs of the group before your own personal needs and goals. This ability involves managing your own feelings, thoughts, and behavior and being able to interpret the needs of the group by using your empathy and reality testing skills. After you reflect on all this information, you can decide on an effective response and continue the feedback loop.

The Empathy Edge

We are all human and experience the same emotions. *Empathy* is one's ability to understand and appreciate the thoughts and feelings of others. Reading others' emotions is a skill you can use to connect with others. This kind of connection can give you the edge in interviews and in networking meetings, as well as help you communicate and work with people on the job.

Being empathic involves demonstrating respect and care for others. Respect is about being open to others and their experiences and their differences, such as different points of view or different cultural beliefs. When you are sensitive to others' needs, you show care and concern. As a result, the people you show empathy to feel cared for and understood. This feeling increases their connection to you and makes them see you as more likeable. However, being empathic doesn't mean that you can't express an opinion. You can disagree with people while showing respect and caring for them.

When you make a conscious effort to think about how another person feels in a situation and you use this information in your interaction (remember the feedback loop), you increase your ability to connect with that person. In Chapter 1, the EQ Exercise "Identify What Makes a Boss Likeable" clarified that emotionally intelligent leaders show through their actions that they value employees both as people and for the work that they do. When employees feel valued and appreciated, they are happier in their jobs, and this feeling leads to increased productivity and better performance.

How do you become more empathic? First, you must be able to identify your own emotions and how they affect your behavior. Knowing your emotions well helps you to become skilled at recognizing and understanding emotions in other people. In other words, you must be self-aware in order to be socially aware. Here are some other things you can do to develop empathy:

- Improve your ability to read body language. Tune into facial expressions, tone of voice, and body posture. What do they tell you about how a person is feeling? (See Table 5.1.)

- Practice active listening by paraphrasing back what you hear someone say to confirm that you heard the person correctly. Try this technique in an interview or networking meeting to ensure clear communication. Practice with family or friends first until you are comfortable with it.

- Ask others to share their thoughts and feelings. When they do, accept their responses without feeling that you have to fix things for them. Just acknowledging that you understand their feelings shows you respect them.

- Practice seeing things from another person's perspective. If you were in that person's situation, how would you feel? What would you think? What would your behavior be like? How can this knowledge help you to better respond to this person?

- Show gratitude and give praise when appropriate. Thank the interviewer for his time. Tell the receptionist that she is doing a good job greeting people and welcoming them to the company (only if this is true, of course). Just as you feel good when you are thanked or given genuine praise, others appreciate these actions, too.

- Express your message without judging others. When you are networking or in an interview, share your view or belief, but do it in a way that welcomes discussion and other ideas.

TABLE 5.1. BODY LANGUAGE AND EMOTIONS

Common Body Signals	Possible Emotions They Convey
Smiling	Confident, optimistic
Firm handshake	Confident, energetic

Common Body Signals	Possible Emotions They Convey
Good eye contact	Honest, interested, engaged
Avoiding eye contact	Dishonest, insecure, nervous
Good posture	Confident, alert
Slouching in seat	Insecure, disinterested
Playing with pen	Nervous, restless
Low or quiet voice tone	Insecure, shy
Bold voice tone	Confident

EMOTIONAL INTELLIGENCE IN ACTION

Bill excelled in college, earning a high GPA and many honors, and now works as an accountant. He is ambitious and feels that there is not much room for advancement in his current company, so he applies for a job at the large, prestigious accounting firm of XYZ & Associates. The firm's human resources manager, who calls Bill to arrange an interview, is impressed with Bill's credentials and tells him that his pre-employment test scores are the highest on record. When Bill arrives for his interview with Luis, the hiring manager, he is feeling confident and excited.

While waiting outside Luis's office, Bill notices small groups of people talking quietly amongst themselves. He is curious, but he decides to stay focused on his upcoming interview instead of trying to socialize. Bill is determined not to let any of the commotion affect his performance. When the interview begins, Luis apologizes, "I'm sorry if I seem distracted. This morning I had to call an ambulance to take an employee who was having chest pains to the hospital."

Even though Luis is clearly upset by the day's events, Bill decides to push on to the task at hand by pointing out his stellar employment record and mastery of accounting. Luis is bothered by the fact that Bill doesn't acknowledge the day's events, sympathize with the effects on Luis, or show any concern for the sick employee. Everyone in Luis's department gets along well, and Bill seems too focused on himself. Although Bill is qualified, Luis believes Bill's lack of concern for others will cause him to have problems with his coworkers. Bill's only concern seems to be getting this job. By the end of the interview, Luis decides that Bill is "not a fit."

(continued)

(continued)

Bill does not get the job offer because he displays low emotional intelligence and, in particular, lacks empathy. He doesn't seem to be able to see the situation from Luis's point of view. If Bill could step back from his own needs in that moment and express concern and understanding for Luis's situation, he would make a better connection with Luis. He would also be perceived as a caring person and as someone positive to have in the company.

Using Empathy to Choose a Career

Empathy is taking on another perspective or imagining what it would be like to be in another person's position. By combining this skill with the creative visualization technique you learned about in Chapter 2, you can try on different careers. Picture yourself in the career that you are considering. What images come to mind? What would you be doing? What kind of environment would you be working in? What kinds of people would you be dealing with? Do you enjoy envisioning yourself in this role? If this exercise is difficult for you, you may need to do more research about that career (through books and the Internet, job shadowing and internships, and information interviews) to be able to fill in the details.

Of course, empathy is not so much a part of the process of choosing a career as it is a part of the career that you choose. Certain occupations require individuals to have high levels of empathy in order to be successful. For example, professions in health care and in the helping fields, such as nurses, dentists, doctors, physical therapists, and counselors, require a significant amount of understanding and compassion. Careers in teaching and training also require the ability to put yourself in your students' shoes and come up with a teaching plan to best help the students learn. Politicians need empathy to understand the people whom they represent and their needs in their communities; those who do not express empathy have shorter political careers.

As mentioned in Chapter 1, empathy also is important in professions that involve sales or customer service. In order to sell a product, a salesperson first has to know the needs of the customer. Salespeople find out this information by being good listeners and communicators, both of which entail empathy.

If empathy is not your strong point, consider choosing an occupation that involves working mainly with information, such as a statistician or scientist, or equipment, such as an engineer or computer programmer, instead of one that involves working with people most of the time.

Whatever job you choose, however, empathy will be helpful for success. You will likely work as part of a team, and developing empathy skills can improve your communication and interaction with others so that you can work more effectively on a project. You also will have a manager whom you will need to get along with, and having empathy will help you understand the business from his perspective and what he expects from you in your job. Suppose your boss is told by the president of the company that he has to increase sales margins by a set date or jobs will be cut. Your boss takes that message to you by telling you that you need to work more efficiently or there will be serious consequences for everyone. When you use empathy, you have a broader understanding of the pressure and stress that your boss is under that trickles down to you. You might then try to work with him instead of argue with or oppose him because you understand the situation and its potential impact on you.

Using Empathy to Find the Right Job

One important component of empathy is being a good listener and communicator. As you network with others to gather information about jobs and opportunities, concentrate on listening to others and even repeat back or summarize what their message is to make sure you understood it accurately. When you are listening to an interviewer, sometimes other thoughts creep in, such as what question you want to ask next, that make it difficult for you to listen well. Stay focused! You need to be able to clarify what the interviewer is telling you about the position. Clear communication is critical when you are making decisions about your future job.

When you are considering a particular job, try the visualization technique described in the preceding section. Do you fit into the industry? Can you picture yourself in this particular job? Do you fit into the company? Can you picture yourself working with the people you have met in your interviews? What would it be like working in this location and taking the commute each day? This information can help you in deciding whether a particular job is the right one for you.

Using Empathy to Get the Job Offer

Getting the job offer hinges on your performance in the interview, which is dependent on how well you connect with the interviewer. Genuinely listening to the interviewer and showing interest and understanding through your comments and questions will help build a connection. The following responses are examples of how you can show empathy in an interview.

Interviewer's Comment	Your Empathic Response
"Sorry that I am late. We are short-handed right now, and I am wearing too many hats."	"It sounds like you are very busy. I hope I will have the opportunity to take some of those tasks off your hands."
"I have only 30 minutes for this interview, so let's get started."	"I understand your time limitation, and I will keep my answers brief, so we can maximize your time."
"Give me a minute to review your resume. I did not get a chance to look it over ahead of time."	"Take your time. It sounds like you are quite busy. I can provide some major highlights for you if you wish after you finish your review."

In any interaction or relationship, both parties must act in order for a connection to be made. If one person fails to reach out, the connection will not happen. When you interview for a job, you can only do your part in making the connection. You can influence the interviewer, but you have no control over him or her. So focus on yourself. To connect with an interviewer, first reflect on your thoughts, feelings, and behaviors while being socially aware of the interviewer and the job interview situation. You then need to make conscious choices on how to best manage yourself in order to get the interviewer to see you as a likeable person. To seal your status and support your case for being the best candidate for the position, communicate your education, experience, skills, and so forth.

EMOTIONAL INTELLIGENCE IN ACTION

Howard has a job interview with Mrs. Perez. He is anxious, and he shows it from the moment he sits down in her office. He has stiff mannerisms and answers questions in a serious, monotone voice. He asks a lot of questions (too many, in fact), but he doesn't smile at all or display a trace of humor.

Mrs. Perez finds Howard difficult to talk to. As the interview continues, she wishes someone would rescue her from the situation so that she could move on to more pleasant tasks. Howard is so focused on listing his qualifications that he does not notice that Mrs. Perez has lost interest. By not connecting with her, he pushes himself further from getting the job. Ultimately, Mrs. Perez decides not to offer Howard the job even though he meets the criteria.

Reality Testing: Sizing Up the Job Market

Do you seem to know what is going on and have an accurate handle on it? Or do you often feel out of touch, like you are missing the signals around you? In the explanation of the EQ Connection Triangle in Chapter 2, you learned that you have to be able to assess thoughts realistically and accurately to affect your emotions and behavior in a positive way. This assessment is using the emotional intelligence skill of reality testing. *Reality testing* is your ability to accurately evaluate the immediate situation. It entails determining how much of what you are feeling and experiencing (which is subjective information) relates to what is objectively happening.

The more aware you are of others' behaviors, the environment, and the politics in a current situation, the better able you can manage yourself in dealing with all of them in a constructive way. An accurate assessment of others and the environment can then lead to an accurate assessment of options. In this way, reality testing is an important component of problem solving. (Adaptability also plays a part in the problem-solving process, as explained in the chapter on self-management skills, Chapter 4.) You have to see the situation clearly before you can come up with options and choose an effective solution.

EQ EXERCISE: IMPROVE YOUR JOB SEARCH REALITY TESTING

In order to get objective information to support what you are thinking and feeling about your job search, you must be able to get input from others whom you respect and trust. If there are some discrepancies between what you think and what they think, you can look at them, gather information, and make some changes.

Start taking stock of how your job search is progressing by asking yourself these questions:

1. How do you know you have a good resume? Does what you think about your resume match what others think of it?

2. Have you selected your target positions and industries by doing research? Does the information you have support your choices?

3. Is the way you have been looking for a job effective? Talk with others about what is working and not working for them. Share your thoughts.

4. What are your interviewing strengths and weaknesses? Role-play interviews with friends or family members and ask them to give you feedback on your interviewing skills.

5. Have you researched the company that you will be interviewing with? You need to know about the company to be prepared for the interview. You also want to find out if the company is a match for you and what you want.

6. Have you done your research to see whether the salary you expect is realistic for the kind of job you are targeting? Web sites such as www.salary.com can assist you with this research.

7. When considering a job offer, have you listed the pros and cons? Have you asked others for their thoughts and feelings about your offer and situation?

8. Do you fit into the company culture? Have you talked to people who are currently working for or have worked for that company to gather this information? What do you still need to know?

Using Reality Testing to Choose a Career

Strong reality testing can be an important factor to being successful in certain jobs. Sales and marketing professionals need to be in tune with the needs and changes in the marketplace. Doctors, nurses, and other medical professionals need to deal with the real data and sort out all the other stuff that can get in the way of making an accurate diagnosis.

Reality testing also is an important skill to use when choosing your career. Think about all that a career involves and whether it is a career that you would enjoy and one that would meet your needs. Look at the facts about the requirements for that career, such as levels of experience, education, cognitive intelligence, and emotional intelligence. Reflect on your skills using your self-awareness and honesty and compare it with the reality of what is needed to be successful in that career. Is there a match?

For example, if you know you cannot sing well and that you are not musically inclined, then you will want to stay away from careers in music. You may want to be a professional pilot, but if you do not have 20/20 vision, this goal is not realistic. CEOs of large companies need a certain level of cognitive intelligence and interpersonal skills to be effective. If this is your goal, do you have enough of these skills to be effective in such a role? Have you received feedback from your past managers to support this career goal?

Sometimes reality testing helps to define which career goals are long-term and which are achievable in the short term. For example, if you are a new college graduate in business who wants to be an entrepreneur, you more than likely need to build money or assets first and obtain hands-on experience working in the business world before you can be successful with your own business. You can use your reality testing and decide to work as an assistant manager for a small business for a couple years to gain experience and acquire money for the long-term goal of having your own business. In the meantime, you can also build relationships with possible investors.

Using Reality Testing to Find the Right Job

To match up your skills and interests with particular jobs in particular industries, you must accurately size up the job market and understand what the actual opportunities are and assess what the likelihood is that you will find one that fits. Books and Internet resources can provide projected information on the growth of certain occupations and the number of new jobs expected annually in that position. One such resource is the United States

Department of Labor Web site at www.bls.gov. This site provides valuable information on the changing trends in the job market and in various industries. It reports the top 10 growing occupations and gives information on jobs that are becoming extinct. You would be wise to stay away from declining occupations and industries. If you decide to target a job on the decline, then use your reality testing to know and accept the fact that the odds are not in your favor and that you may be searching for a longer time for such a position.

Strong reality testing is reliant on effective information gathering. When you prepare for interviews, you can gather information through networking to help you decide whether a certain company or job is right for you. Start by asking your friends and family if they know anyone who works at the company. If they do, get a name and number so that you can talk to the person. Emphasize the fact that you are not asking the person to put in a good word for you; you are just looking for information to help you decide whether this company will be the right fit for you. When you talk to company employees, ask about their likes and dislikes about their job and the company. During job interviews, you should also ask questions so that you can ascertain what it would be like to work at the job on a day-to-day basis.

Another way to connect with employees in companies that you are interested in is LinkedIn, a growing social networking Internet site at www.linkedin.com. Unlike more purely social sites such as Facebook, LinkedIn keeps the focus on business. It is based on the idea that relationships can be a valuable asset in making good connections in your job search and career. LinkedIn allows you to create a public profile and to link to colleagues and friends whom you currently know. Once you are connected to them, you can view their connections, which thus expands your network and allows you to contact people whom you are interested in talking with.

EMOTIONAL INTELLIGENCE IN ACTION

Shreya is looking for a company that she will be happy working for. In order to achieve this, she looks for an engineering job in a company that shares the same values as hers. She values work/life balance and wants a job mainly to support herself and her hobbies and interests outside of work. She does not want to work long hours or travel. A prestigious company has offered her a large salary and sign-on bonus but states that the job involves traveling 50 percent of the time, including some weekends. She is honored and excited by the offer from the well-known company and loves the idea of making a huge salary. She tells herself that maybe it won't be 50 percent travel and that possibly she could get by with less. She tries to convince herself that she can pursue her hobbies on the road even though that would be inconvenient.

Is Shreya being honest with herself? No. She is not using her emotional intelligence to make the best decision for herself. She is twisting the reality of the situation and distorting the data to make the situation fit. Accepting the reality that this high-paying job will not work for her and that she needs to turn down the offer is difficult. However, short-term unhappiness is better than the long-term unhappiness that may come from finding herself stuck one year from now in a job that she hates. Accepting reality and using it to make a good decision while accepting and managing the uncomfortable feelings that her decision brings is acting with emotional intelligence.

Using Reality Testing to Negotiate the Job Offer

Knowing what you want out of your next job before you start interviewing can provide the structure and guidance that is needed to make a good decision. After acknowledging a job offer, you need to decide whether you will accept the terms of the offer as it stands or whether you will negotiate any of the terms such as the number of weeks of vacation or your starting date. For some jobs, negotiation is not an option. Certain government positions, for example, are bound by strict standards and guidelines as to pay and benefits. Certain entry-level jobs are also set. Using your reality testing involves researching whether the terms of the job offer can be negotiated. You might also choose not to negotiate because you are aware that you are not a strong negotiator and you do not want to negatively impact your beginning relationship with your new employer.

If you decide to negotiate, arm yourself with information. Use networking and research to figure out realistic salary ranges for the position you are offered. There should be some basis for the salary amount that you ask for. Also, talk with a significant other or a mentor to sound off about what your concerns and needs are and do a practice negotiation.

Be realistic in knowing what the company can give. Companies are working under tight budgets and guidelines in today's economy. You may think you are the best thing since sliced bread, but the reality is that there are others who also can do the same job. Do not let your emotions cloud your judgment or get in the way. Do not make the mistake of being too proud or too confident and expect that employers are going to pay you a huge salary.

Social Responsibility

Social responsibility is your involvement in the community and willingness to work with others for the common good of the group or organization. Being involved in your community shows you are well-rounded and have this skill. Some companies value social responsibility and want assurance that you can look beyond your personal needs to your team's or organization's needs and goals. Businesses want to know you are willing to go the extra mile for their company. You are expected to put business needs before personal needs.

Companies look for employees who can act independently but also work well as part of a team toward the same or related goals. A person who is too independent can become so isolated from other team members that he no longer works well with them.

EMOTIONAL INTELLIGENCE IN ACTION

Debbie has been out of work for eight months. She is an accountant and lost her position due to a company merger. Although she has been working hard and feels that her job search is going well, she also feels isolated and unproductive by not having a job to go to each day. She decides to join a job search networking group to share her talents with others and to gain support in return. She volunteers to be the group's treasurer.

When she interviews for jobs and the interviewers ask what she has been doing with her time while in career transition, she shares that she is part of a job search support group and volunteers her time and talents. The employer who later hires Debbie tells her that her social responsiveness and commitment to others were important in his decision to hire her. The employer also decides to advertise future job openings in his company on the job search networking group's Web site in order to recruit more socially responsive applicants.

EQ EXERCISE: DEVELOP SOCIAL RESPONSIBILITY FOR THE JOB SEARCH

Answer the following questions in the space provided.

What strengths and talents can you share with others?

_____

_____

_____

_____

How can you be more socially responsible in your personal life? Is there a way you can help others? Are you willing to volunteer in a community organization?

_____

_____

_____

How can you make a difference at your current company (if you are still employed)? How can you build an atmosphere of concern and cooperation at work?

_____

_____

_____

_____

Using Social Responsibility to Choose a Career

As with empathy, the skill of social responsibility should be considered in the type of career that you choose. If you know working for the good of the community or with diverse groups of people is a strength and interest for you, you should seek out careers that involve cultural relations and social responsibility, such as a community organizer, urban planner, foreign correspondent, public administrator, or public relations specialist.

Volunteering is also a good way to learn about a career and to gain experience. You help others and at the same time help yourself by experiencing what is involved in working in that career.

Using Social Responsibility to Find the Right Job

Some companies are more actively involved in community programs than others. If social responsibility is important to you, look for a company that integrates socially responsible programs into its business. The book *The Job Seeker's Guide to Socially Responsible Companies* by Katherine Jankowski may be helpful to you in exploring companies who focus on giving back to the community and accept and encourage it as part of their company culture. Some companies might offer nontraditional work schedules such as working from home one day a week in support of work/life balance. Some will allow you to take considerable work time to participate in charity events that support their mission and vision.

Networking involves social responsibility in that, when you network, it is not all about you getting what you want. Networking is also about supporting people whom you are networking with. You are asking for information for yourself to assess whether a certain occupation, job, or company is right for you. You also share information that will be helpful to other people in their business and endeavors. It is in giving of yourself that you will feel good about taking in return.

For example, when I was making the transition from a counselor in the educational system to a career coach in the business sector, I met with a continuous quality improvement manager at a career and vocational college. I shared information about my interest in teaching emotional intelligence skills to her staff and teaching career education to students. I asked her questions about opportunities in her college and in the community. She in turn asked me about my knowledge of certain career assessments. I gave her information on those assessments and how to access them.

Networking groups can be very helpful in your job search. These groups are formed so that people with a common goal can support each other through the stressful process of finding a job. Individuals share their diverse experience and knowledge to help each other. You have the opportunity to get names of individuals to network with by sharing names of people you know with other group members. There are many diverse kinds of groups. There are groups in which members all have the same target occupation, such as information technology or finance. There are also general job search groups in which professionals from diverse occupations come together to support and assist one another.

Many cities have job search networking groups. One source for finding networking groups in your area is www.job-hunt.org, which taps into various kinds of networking groups by location.

Using Social Responsibility to Get the Job Offer

Being socially responsible might not win you the job offer, but it adds to your resume and shows that you are a well-rounded individual who can look beyond himself to the concerns of the greater good. If the employer values this quality, it will give you an edge.

At the end of your resume, you can add an optional section that lists community involvement. List the organization, positions held, years of service, and any accomplishments that showcase your skills. Do not dilute your resume with too much community involvement or with activities that are not directly related to your target job. For example, if you are seeking a teaching or training position, it is a good idea to list Junior Achievement, in which you taught business programs to high school students on a volunteer basis. However, you would not list the fact that you compile statistics for your son's baseball team because it is not relevant and does not add more value.

Social responsibility is a trait that is often used in screening and selection. For example, colleges screen applicants for admission by looking at a student's record of community service. Companies will screen college graduate applicants by using social responsibility. Many college graduates look alike on paper with similar majors and grades, so related job experience (internships), leadership positions, and community involvement is what sets them apart from others.

If a company is looking for candidates who support its value of community involvement and social responsibility, and you do not display this value or interest, you might be ruled out of the selection process. If you want the job and like the company and know that social responsibility is important, communicate your desire and motivation to get involved during the interview, and then, of course, do it.

You shouldn't bring up too many personal wants, needs, and dislikes in an interview. Employers are looking for team players who focus on the organization. When an employer offers you the job, you can address specific personal issues such as needing time off for a vacation that has already been paid for. You have the most influence at this point because the employer has decided he wants you and thus is more likely to be willing to work with you.

Don't think you can't ask questions, however. You should ask questions throughout the interview process to check out responsibilities and expectations of the job. Don't wait until you have the job offer to start asking questions about travel, overtime, and so on. Certainly if the interviewer asks questions about any area that is a concern for you, you should be honest and deal with the matter at that point in time. For example, if the potential employer asks if you are willing to travel out of town on weekends, and you know you cannot do this, be upfront with the employer. Don't expect to negotiate this term at the time of an offer.

Role Models with High Social Awareness

Many individuals devote much time and hard work to improve the world around them. For example, actor Angelina Jolie and rock star Bono help impoverished communities access resources. One person whom I admire who has very strong social awareness skills is past Secretary of State Condoleezza Rice. She has a keen ability to listen, understand, and communicate with people of different cultures and with people of different status in those cultures. Through her genuineness, honesty, and empathy, she develops and maintains good working relationships with people of different countries around the world. She is able to assess situations accurately and realistically and works towards the goal of supporting democracy around the world.

Personally, the best role model for the social awareness skill of empathy was my mother. She modeled it for me and my sisters through her interaction with others. She was very good at reading others and at communicating in a down-to-earth way with just about anybody. She was genuine and sensitive and helped others without thinking about payment in return.

I have worked with several clients who are involved extensively in community service and have documented this work on their resumes. These well-rounded professionals show a balanced perspective through their actions. Through their involvement with community organizations, they demonstrate that they can look beyond their personal circumstances to work for the good of others. They add to the community and environment around them instead of just take from it.

Chapter Reflections

Social awareness starts with taking in data or information, both about others and their emotions as well as about the environment, and then making a choice on how to respond based on your interpretation of the data. Reading the data accurately will lead to a more effective response. The feedback loop helps you to understand how we affect and are affected by others. As you might remember from the Introduction, the skills in social awareness are particularly important in stage II (exploring career options) and stage III (targeting specific jobs and careers) of the career transition process.

The skill of empathy is one's ability to understand and appreciate the thoughts and feelings of others by observing what they say and do. Empathy is very important in the kind of occupation that you choose because some require you to be highly empathic to be successful. Empathy is important in an interview to assess the interviewer's emotions in that moment and use it to guide your response. The interview is about making a connection, and empathy is the skill that can enable you to create the connection through active listening and communication.

Where empathy is the ability to read a person, reality testing is the ability to accurately read a situation. An accurate assessment of others and the environment will lead to accurately assessing options and to choosing the best way to respond. Reality testing in the job search involves getting accurate information and using it as a guide to target the right job. You want to match up your skills and interests with the right job or position in the right industry. Knowing what you want out of your next job before you start interviewing can provide the structure and guidance you need when you have to make a decision on whether to accept a job offer and whether to negotiate any of the terms of the offer.

The third skill in social awareness is social responsibility, which is your involvement in the community and willingness to work with others for the common good of the group and organization. Companies look for individuals who create a positive company culture, who add value and contribute, and who demonstrate a commitment to working with others toward a common goal. Companies also want someone who is independent but can balance this with being a good team player. If social responsibility is very important to you, you will want to find a company that integrates socially responsive programs into its business.

You now understand how using your self-awareness and social awareness can help you maneuver yourself to interact with others and your environment effectively. In the next chapter, you will learn how to interact with others by using the social skills that are a part of emotional intelligence.

CHAPTER 6

Social Skills: Communicate and Collaborate to Succeed in the Job Search

You can have good self-awareness and social awareness and manage your emotions well, yet you still need to effectively interact and communicate with others in order to achieve the outcomes you want. If you have good social skills, you may take them for granted. They work for you and help you to achieve your goals and have satisfying relationships. However, when you do not have these skills to an adequate degree, you experience problems interacting with people, both at work and in your personal life.

The emotional intelligence area of social skills covers the skills necessary to develop and maintain relationships and to work with others. The area of social skills is composed of the following five skills or competencies:

- Honesty, integrity, and trust

- Communication and assertiveness

- Cooperation, collaboration, and teamwork

- Conflict management and negotiation

- Influence on and development of others

There is a hierarchy involved in these social skills (see Figure 6.1). Some of the social skills, such as communication, are simpler and less complex and thus easier to develop and use. The more complex skills, such as conflict negotiation, build on the simpler skills. You need to start from the simpler skills and work up. As you read through this chapter, it is helpful to understand how this social skills hierarchy is formed and to assess what your level of skill is at this time.

Figure 6.1. The hierarchy of social skills.

This chapter will help you assess what your strengths and weak areas are in social skills and will provide exercises to develop these skills. As I have in the past three chapters, I also will share how you can use these skills more fully to enhance every aspect of your job search and career.

Trust: The Foundation of a Successful Career

Honesty, integrity, and trust are the most basic of the social skills and are necessary for success. These qualities are often abbreviated as H.I.T.: Honesty, Integrity, and Trust. A person who acts honestly and becomes trustworthy is seen as someone who has integrity. He cares about himself and others and shows it in his actions.

We expect honesty from others and are disappointed when it is absent. We see the damaging effects of dishonesty when corporate executives steal money from their stockholders or when politicians participate in illegal activities. Our expectation is that these people of public responsibility would exhibit strong interpersonal skills, integrity, and service to others, and when they do not, feelings of betrayal and anger abound.

You have already chosen by now in your life whether you are going to live in an honest way. It is almost impossible to behave honestly at home and then dishonestly at work or vice versa. Honesty is a value and becomes a habit and runs through all areas of your life. As spiritual author Matthew Kelly said in his book *Rediscovering Catholicism,* "Your habits form your character, and your character is your destiny."

Do what you say you are going to do each and every time. People then know they can count on you (notice that *count* is in the word *accountability*). When you fail to do what you say you are going to do, take responsibility for the consequences. Taking responsibility can be difficult, but admitting failure or mistakes and accepting the negative outcome is necessary to hold on to your accountability and integrity. It shows that you know you messed up and you are going to make a change or correct it so it does not happen again. The goal is to learn from it and move on. Matthew Kelly's *Book of Courage* has the following quote from Michael Jordan that illustrates this point:

> *"I've missed more than 9,000 shots in my career. I've lost more than 300 games, and 26 times I've been trusted to take the game-winning shot and missed. Throughout my life and career, I've failed and failed and failed again. And that is why I succeed."*

Using H.I.T. to Choose a Career

Being honest is crucial from the beginning to the end of the job search. In any occupation that you choose, you need to be honest. And the person you most need to be honest with is yourself. When choosing a career, make sure it is what you want to do and not something that your parents or others have persuaded you to do. Remember that your values and beliefs drive your behavior, and if you are not in a profession for the right reasons, you will become unhappy and dissatisfied, which can affect your productivity and performance on the job.

Using H.I.T. to Find the Right Job

Not only do you need to be honest with yourself in choosing the right career, but also in finding the right job to apply for. Suppose that you decided you wanted to be a teacher, and now upon graduation you have to find the job. Self-awareness and social awareness come in to play again to help you figure out the environment and/or community you want to teach in. There are many different environments to choose from: private or public school, urban or suburban setting, culturally homogeneous or ethnically diverse schools, and so on. You have to be honest with yourself in knowing what is best for you, your interests, and your needs. Your comfort and satisfaction in your job setting will affect your success.

Using H.I.T. to Get the Job Offer

The job interview is about building the relationship between you and the potential employer, and all healthy relationships start with and are based on trust. Trust is the foundation for continued interactions. People get a sense of whether they can trust you from how you handle yourself. Start with a firm handshake and look the interviewer in the eyes as you communicate to convey your trustworthiness. If you look down a lot or shift your eyes away from the interviewer when you answer questions, he may interpret that to mean that you are being dishonest. (If you *are* dishonest in the interview or on your resume and get hired, you risk losing your job if the issue is later uncovered. Once you are dishonest, you will have a difficult time being hired by someone else.)

If you talk with honesty and integrity, and do not put on airs, the potential employer will obtain a sense that you are genuine. He can believe what you say and will hire you for the job because you present yourself as someone whom he can rely on and trust to do the job.

Doug Hall, in his book *Jump Start Your Business Brain*, describes the three traits needed to be successful in marketing yourself or your product: overt benefit, real reason to believe, and dramatic difference. I use the initials BCD to remember these traits: benefit, credibility, and difference. When you market yourself in an interview, you have to communicate the benefit you bring to an employer with regard to your skills, education, and experience. The second trait of credibility is all about honesty, integrity, and trust. You have to convince the interviewer to believe in you and trust in you. Through what you say and how you say it, you make a connection and build a relationship with the interviewer with the goal that he will decide that he can trust you to do the job and to do it well. The interviewer is also assessing whether by hiring you the job responsibilities will be fulfilled. He wants to know that hiring you will make a difference.

Clear and Assertive Communication: A Must in the Job Market

Communication is about sending and receiving messages, and the better you do this, the more accurate information you have and the more effective the interaction can be. Communicating your thoughts clearly and confidently while taking into account others' perspectives will lead to quality interactions.

In order to become skilled at communication, one has to be a good sender as well as receiver. Think about your speaking skills. If you can answer yes to all of the following questions, you probably are a good sender. If not, you need to improve your sending skills.

- When you speak, do you send messages in a clear way?

- Do you speak with clear pronunciation and a strong voice tone?

- Do you deliver your message in a timely way?

- Do you give examples when others need clarification?

To practice your sending skills, ask others in your day-to-day conversations whether they understand what you say. Ask them to repeat the message back to you in their own words. This way you can see whether the message was indeed received correctly. You can even tell them you are working on improving your communication skills and ask them if they have any feedback that might be helpful to you.

In order to be a good receiver, you must be a good listener. You have to be able to tune in to what others are saying and then reflect on understanding their message.

Note that there are two parts to every message:

- **Content:** What the message says—the meaning of the words.

- **Process:** How the message is delivered. This includes physical cues, such as such as facial expressions, body posture, voice tone, and pace of speech, as well as choice of words.

Examining both content and process in communication provides rich information, thus increasing your social awareness.

To improve your listening skills, confirm the accuracy of what you hear by restating what others say and checking it out with them for accuracy. In my work, I often say, "So to clarify what you said, you think …," or "So if I heard you correctly, you are saying that…."

When you communicate openly and assertively, you stand up for yourself and your rights. This kind of communication ultimately can bring you closer to your goals and satisfaction. Note that assertive communication is when you express your thoughts and feelings (both positive and negative) in a constructive way that shows respect for others who are involved. In contrast, aggressive communication happens when a person expresses his thoughts and feelings at the expense of another in a harmful or abusive way.

Communication and assertiveness go back to using your self-awareness and social awareness to know what to communicate—the content—and how to communicate it—the process. Put the thoughts-feelings-behavior connection into action. In order to express yourself accurately, you have to be clear about your needs and the situation. You do this by reflecting on your thoughts and feelings. To communicate effectively, you have to choose to communicate at a good time for everyone involved. The behavior part of this process is using your words, your actions, and your writing to get your message across.

Using Communication and Assertiveness to Choose a Career

Some occupations require stronger communication skills than others. For example, salespeople, whether they are selling insurance or selling machines, must be strong communicators in order to be successful in building relationships and influencing and persuading others to purchase products. If you choose to go into social work, teaching, or law, you will need strong verbal communication skills to do your job effectively. Verbal communication skills are not as critical to success in occupations such as information technology in which the work is focused on systems and software.

Some occupations require more indirect forms of communication skills, such as writing or artistic expression. Careers in journalism or technical writing require excellent writing skills. Careers in architecture, graphic design, and advertising require artistic expression and the ability to communicate through different mediums.

With regard to assertiveness, being able to express yourself openly is critical to success in particular professions. Lawyers, politicians, ministers and other religious workers, business consultants, and any position in a management role are all careers in which you have to stand up and express viewpoints and manage opposition. Being able to interact with others in these roles takes strong communication skills. In contrast, occupations such as an interior designer or a carpenter likely do not need a high amount of assertiveness. These professionals work to assist others on their projects.

Using Communication and Assertiveness to Find the Right Job

Sitting back and waiting for someone to respond to the resumes that you posted on Internet job sites is not an effective way to find a job. Networking is how most people find work. In order to network, you need to communicate with people in the business that you are interested in and with people in your community. This kind of communication takes assertiveness and persistence. You have to ask for what you want.

Before you meet or talk to a networking contact, think about what you want to learn from the person and how you can best ask your questions. Practice asking questions out loud at home. Look in a mirror as you do this to see how you come across.

As you talk to people about your job search, they will give you ideas and leads. If you are networking with a lot of people, you might start to feel overwhelmed with all the suggestions and feedback. To handle the information effectively, follow these steps:

1. Step back and evaluate how the information fits in with what you have already learned about the business, industry, or company.

2. Use your self-awareness to focus on what you want.

3. Decide if you should follow up with a lead or perhaps revise your strategy and change your approach based on your new information.

Using Communication and Assertiveness to Get the Job Offer

A job interview is a test of your communication skills. You have to listen openly and communicate back clearly. As you and the potential employer communicate, you are both trying to assess whether there is a fit with you and the job.

Now is the time to demonstrate your assertiveness by expressing yourself and your ideas. Be confident in yourself, and it will show in your answers to the interviewer's questions. Throughout the interview, ask yourself, "Can I meet this organization's needs, and, if so, how will I communicate this?" You have to communicate in a convincing way.

However, be careful to not be too assertive to the point of pushing yourself, your skills, and your views on the interviewer. Pushing is the key word. Think about how you feel when someone tries to push his views on you. You likely feel uncomfortable and maybe intimidated, as if your views don't count or aren't important to that individual. Sometimes when people feel this way, they work to defend their views even more and are thus less open to considering another perspective.

Listen to the interviewer. Show that you understand the interviewer and his situation (and demonstrate your social awareness skills) by acknowledging his concerns and addressing his needs, as opposed to being focused only on what you want him to know about you. If the interviewer questions your answers or approach, reflect on what he is saying and respectfully respond.

You want to communicate your views while also hearing his views. If your answer is in disagreement to the interviewer's thoughts, state what data has led you to your decision.

A job interview isn't just about answering questions; it's about asking them, too. Waiting until the job is offered to you to ask questions is too late. Asking questions during the interview shows that you are trying to make the best decision on your end and displays emotional intelligence.

Use self-talk to help you think about what information you still need to know. For example, you need to find out the duties and expectations for the position. Monitor your feelings throughout the interview as well. Use the information you get from reflecting on these feelings to formulate more questions or pinpoint concerns for the interviewer to address. If the interviewer's responses to your questions are unclear, be assertive and ask for clarification. Before the interview ends, make sure that you have the information you need to make a decision about this job if it is offered to you.

One question you can ask to try to close the deal is, "Do my qualifications fit what you are looking for?" If the response is positive, reinforce your qualifications. If the response is a hesitation or the interviewer brings up an area in which he feels you are lacking, you have an opportunity to change the interviewer's mind with a rebuttal. You might share an additional example or information to make your point. If you are successful, you will be closer to being seriously considered for the position.

When you are offered a position, assertiveness comes into play if you choose to negotiate any of the terms of the job offer, such as salary or vacation. If you feel, based on your skills and experience and from your research, that the employer is offering too low a salary and/or too little vacation, you have choices. You can refuse the offer, you can accept the offer as it stands, or you can speak up and ask the employer to consider a higher salary and/or another week of vacation. Know what the minimum is that you can accept in a new job and use it as your guide. Take into account the employer's side; the employer may have budget constraints or guidelines on new hires that he has to follow. Sometimes employers will hire at a lower figure and agree to review your performance (and consider a raise) after a few months on the job. This arrangement allows you a chance to prove your skills and gives the employer an opportunity to assess your skills.

Cooperation, Collaboration, and Teamwork: The Keys to Maintaining Relationships

Cooperation, collaboration, and teamwork are skills that most of us were taught in elementary school, but some adults struggle to use them effectively. You might have heard someone say about someone else that "he doesn't play nice in the sandbox," meaning that he is lacking in social skills. When you have to work with these kinds of people, you may become frustrated because they seem like obstacles instead of teammates.

In order to build solid working relationships, you need to practice the skills of cooperation and collaboration. They do not come easily or automatically. Saying whatever is on your mind is not the most emotionally intelligent approach. Being emotionally intelligent is going through the process of reflecting on your thoughts and feelings (self-awareness) and then making a choice on what you are going to say and do (self-management) based on your inner reflection as well as your assessment of the situation and the people involved (social awareness). You can see that in order to master the social skill of collaborating and working on a team, you need a good grip on the skills in the other three EQ areas.

Think about how you show cooperation. Do you demonstrate it in your actions as well as in your words? Sometimes people say they want to cooperate and work together, but their actions show otherwise. They may show opposition or defiance by saying they will do something but not following through on their words. Think about your style in your past jobs. Do you show a cooperative, can-do attitude? Do you show it in job interviews by what you say and how you say it?

Collaboration involves sharing your ideas and listening to and using the ideas of others. Do you ask others for their opinions and draw them into the conversation? In job interviews and networking meetings, the goal is to ask questions and get information as well as to share your ideas. Are you talking too much and not listening enough?

In order to cooperate and collaborate with others, you have to tame your independence. Independence is a self-management skill that is used effectively when you act in a way that takes into account both internal information (self-awareness) and external information (social awareness). When you are working on your own or doing your part of a group project, you need independence in order to take action without being overly concerned about getting others' approval. However, when you come into a team meeting, you want to tame your independence to collaborate and cooperate and fit your part of the project into the whole. Depending on the situation, you will need to act more independently or more cooperatively to be the most effective in achieving the overall outcome.

EMOTIONAL INTELLIGENCE IN ACTION

Samir is beginning a new job as a project engineer on a multimillion-dollar bridge project. One of the reasons he was hired is that he impressed his manager by sharing his experience and skills in working on a similar project in another state. He is eager to share his expertise with his new team as well.

During his first days on the job, he learns others' views and expectations of him and his role and communicates his thoughts. Because he is new, the other members of his team do not want to manage the project in the way he suggests. They want to keep the power and do things the way they always have.

Samir feels frustrated because he believes his way would be successful if they would be open to it. He also knows that the team has not been fully effective in the past and that his manager liked his ideas when he was hired (social awareness). He reflects on his feelings of frustration and on the situation (self-awareness) and decides how to act. Samir tells the team that he knows he is new to their organization and respects the way that they have done things in the past. However, he goes on to say (assertiveness) that he can add some value to the team and to this project because of his past failures (honesty and genuineness) as well as his past successes on similar projects. He states that he wants to work with them on their plans but hopes that they can be open to some of his ideas and experience as they move forward (cooperation and collaboration). He states that the ultimate goal is for this project to be successful (social responsibility).

Samir acts with all areas of his emotional intelligence, which leads the team to accepting him more openly and agreeing to try some of his ideas. The team members also point out which areas they would not be willing to change, and Samir accepts this. Samir has made progress in his new work relationships, which hopefully will contribute to a successful project outcome.

EQ EXERCISE: ASSESS COOPERATION AND COLLABORATION COMPETENCIES

Rate yourself on the following skills on a scale of 1 to 10, with 10 being very high. Circle the number on the scale that best represents you. Respond in terms of your behavior in your past or current jobs and not with regard to your behavior in personal and family situations.

Independence (your ability to function effectively without direction from others and without being overly concerned about others' reactions)

1   2   3   4   5   6   7   8   9   10

Assertiveness (your ability to express your point of view in an effective and constructive way)

1   2   3   4   5   6   7   8   9   10

Empathy (your ability to appreciate the thoughts and feelings of others)

1   2   3   4   5   6   7   8   9   10

Reality testing (your ability to see the situation for what it is)

1   2   3   4   5   6   7   8   9   10

Adaptability (your ability to change in accordance with your environment and go with the flow without discomfort)

1   2   3   4   5   6   7   8   9   10

Scoring

Numbers in the 6–8 range indicate that you have enough of this EQ skill to be cooperative and collaborative. However, having too high of a level, say a 9 or 10, in one of these skills can be a disadvantage when working with others. A number less than 6 signals an area that you might want to develop in order to grow your EQ skills.

Interpretation

This exercise asks you to first be aware of what your qualities are (self-awareness) and then be aware of what the situation is and what others need (social awareness). The next step is to use this information to make a conscious choice on how to act and manage yourself in a way to achieve your goals and the desired outcome. Look at the numbers you circled and ask yourself:

- **How independent are you?** Do you show independence when needed? Can you also shift into a collaboration mode when working with others? Your goal is to be able to function on your own without needing too much direction or approval while also being able to collaborate with others. If you are too independent (a 9 or 10), you might act without considering the other people involved, and this can lead you to become isolated from others. When you have to make a decision or perform a task at work, you need to be able to judge when you should act independently and when you need to collaborate with and engage others.

- **How assertive are you?** Do you express yourself and stand up for yourself or are you quiet and passive, following along even when you sense that you would like to do something different? Do you express your views and persuade others to listen when you feel and think your plan is the best one? Balance again is important because, in the process of asserting yourself, you do not want to discount others' ideas. This behavior would come across as aggressive and not cooperative.

- **How empathic are you?** You want to be sensitive to others' perspectives. If you cannot accept that others have great ideas and

(continued)

(continued)

that those ideas need consideration, then you might come across as uncaring and aloof. If you are too empathic to the point that you do not share your ideas when you feel strongly about them, then you risk being ineffective and not an active contributor to the team or project.

- **Do you usually read the situation and others correctly?** To accurately perceive situations, you have to be able to take in information from all perspectives. Yet if you scored yourself a 9 or 10 in reality testing, you might get too bogged down in the reality of a situation and have difficulty being hopeful or optimistic. You need optimism to pull yourself out of a difficult or problematic situation because it brings energy and openness to new possibilities.

- **How adaptable are you?** Adaptability is important because it enables you to consider other perspectives and try out different ways of doing things. If you are too adaptable, however, you might have difficulty acting assertively and independently when needed. Think of someone who is too laid-back, almost to the point that he does not seem to care. You may have difficulty counting on him to do his part due to his seeming lack of energy or enthusiasm.

Using Cooperation and Collaboration to Choose a Career

Cooperation and collaboration are essential skills in any career that involves being part of a team. Although every job involves teamwork in some way, some professions count on it. For example, event planners have to collaborate with others in order to arrange and run an event. An office manager has to collaborate with all individuals in an office setting, including both customers and workers, to make sure everything runs smoothly for everyone involved in the business.

On the other side, occupations such as engineers, scientists, and technicians focus on working with materials and processes instead of working with people. But people in these professions are sometimes asked to step up and become project leaders or department managers. This change requires cooperation and collaboration skills in addition to technical skills.

Using Cooperation and Collaboration to Find the Right Job

As mentioned in Chapter 5 and in earlier chapters, networking is the prime way to find jobs. Networking involves cooperation and collaboration. It is a two-way street in which you gather information and potential leads, but you also give back information to help the people helping you. Not everyone gets this idea of networking. Some people are not very cooperative or collaborative, and thus your interactions with them will be brief. Don't get discouraged. Keep trying to connect with people who are willing to connect with you.

Joining a networking support group will allow you to interact with many different kinds of people seeking different jobs. This is a great way to meet lots of people and let them know the positions you are targeting. In this way, you can have several people keeping their eyes and ears open for you as they do their own searching. You share leads and resources with others in the group, and they do the same for you.

But what happens when you are targeting the same positions as other people in your group? You will then need to balance your cooperation and collaboration skills with your competitiveness. Use your EQ skills to reflect on your thoughts-feelings-behavior connections and take in information about the situation and the others involved to make a choice on how best to respond to be most effective in reaching your desired outcome. When you have a particular job lead that you are going to apply for, you would likely choose to not share this lead with a fellow group member who is equally qualified for the position. At this point, it is emotionally intelligent to kick in your competitiveness.

Using Cooperation and Collaboration to Get the Job Offer

In an interview, you will need to show a cooperative and collaborative spirit as well as confidence. Your job is to influence and persuade the interviewer to offer you the job, but this happens in an atmosphere of collaboration in which both sides feel respected. You communicate your cooperative spirit in how you listen, talk, and respond.

In an interview, a potential employer looks for information on what kind of team player you will be as well as what kind of leadership you will show. Both are important and needed to some degree, depending on the actual job position. For team player positions, cooperation and collaboration are key skills. Leadership positions emphasize independence, assertiveness, and reality testing. For any position, the employer may be looking for more of one quality than another.

By accurately reading the situation, you can determine what an employer needs and tailor your responses to interview questions to show off the skills that the employer is looking for. For example, an employer may be looking for someone to take charge of a bad situation in a department while cooperating with other executive staff on larger organizational goals. Another employer may be looking for a total team player who can become a leader in the future, after learning the ways of the company.

All companies are looking for employees who want to support the companies' values and culture. They are looking for someone who can adapt to their organization but also bring in new ideas and needed skill sets and experience. In a job interview, you should aim to confidently express your beliefs and offer your expertise while showing openness and flexibility in regards to the experience and expertise of others. If you come across in the interview as domineering and inflexible, the interviewer will likely be turned off. He may doubt your ability to join the organization and work well as part of the team.

Conflict Management and Negotiation: Helpful Skills for the Job Offer and Beyond

Conflict management and negotiation are higher-level social skills, meaning that they take more effort to refine and are based on developing all the social skills that are lower in the hierarchy. To develop and use conflict management and negotiation skills effectively, you also need a well-developed amount of self-awareness, self-management, and social awareness skills.

All of the previous social skills are important in supporting your ability to deal with conflict:

- Displaying integrity
- Assertively expressing your views with the risk that others will not approve

- Communicating and collaborating to come to a place where you can work together

Many people are uncomfortable with conflict. Your comfort level with conflict likely comes from your family dynamics and from your personality. Before you can improve your conflict management skills, you need to know where you are on the continuum of "comfort with conflict." One way to evaluate this is to ask others how they view your ability to deal with conflict. In addition, you can seek out mentors who handle conflict and differences well and learn from them through observation and discussion.

There is a process of accepting conflict as natural and embracing it, becoming more comfortable with it, and responding to it effectively. One way to approach differences is to think of them as opportunities instead of obstacles. With these thoughts, your feelings will be more positive, and your behavior in a conflict will be more effective (the connection between these three things is shown in the EQ Connection Triangle from Chapter 2). If both sides in a conflict value differences, they can approach a conflict as an opportunity for an even better resolution and solution for everyone.

One of the tools I use in staff development and training to help others understand and appreciate individual differences in the work environment is the Myers-Briggs Type Indicator. This assessment increases self-awareness and social awareness, enabling people to manage their actions and interactions in a more conscious and emotionally intelligent way. This assessment measures people across four dimensions:

1. How they energize themselves
2. How they take in information
3. How they make decisions
4. How they organize their life on a daily basis

Understanding where you and others fit in these dimensions provides you with knowledge you can use to resolve differences with different types of people.

In a negotiation, both sides want to work with someone who is honest. If you feel a person is being dishonest, you are aware that you have lost the negotiation even before you start because you are not starting on equal ground. Communication and assertiveness is needed in order to represent your side. If you go into a negotiation not being clear on what you want and how to say it, or if you go in thinking that you do not have a right to ask for what it is you're asking for, you will not be successful. The nature of negotiation means that there has to be a compromise on both sides. This compromise is a result of both sides cooperating and collaborating to bring about an outcome that is mutually acceptable.

EMOTIONAL INTELLIGENCE IN ACTION

A week after interviewing with a leading medical device manufacturing company, Barry receives a call from the company's hiring manager, who offers him the job of Executive Account Manager. (The hiring manager e-mails the offer in writing to Barry as well.) Barry thanks the manager for the offer and says that he is happy to receive it. He states that he feels his past experience in sales in the pharmaceutical business, as well as his extensive network of relationships in the industry, will enable him to increase company sales. Barry asks if he can have a few days to reflect on the offer, talk with his wife, and decide whether he has additional questions. The hiring manager says that Barry can have until the end of the week to make his decision.

Barry assesses the job and company. He reflects on what his skills, interests, needs, and values are and how they match up with this position. He decides that there are two areas he wants to negotiate with the hiring manager: starting date and salary. He calls the hiring manager and says,

"I am happy to receive this offer. However, before I accept the offer, there are two things I would like to talk with you about. First, you put the starting date as two weeks from Monday. However, I would like to extend it to three weeks, if possible, so that I can carry out a planned trip to Mexico for a Habitat for Humanity church retreat."

The manager agrees to the new starting date and asks him some questions about the trip. Barry continues,

"Thank you for working with me on that. The second item I want to discuss is the salary. You offered me $72,000 base pay, but with my experience and large network of contacts and my research of similar jobs in this area, I really hoped for a base pay of $80,000."

The manager says that he can meet Barry halfway at $76,000, but he can't go any higher due to budget constraints. Barry counters, "With all due respect, is it possible for you to check with your manager to see if the larger salary can be reached?"

The hiring manager says he can do this, although he is not very hopeful that doing so will bring a different outcome. Barry asks whether a sign-on bonus is a possibility instead to carry him to his next performance evaluation. The hiring manager says that he is open to this possibility and that he will check on this and get back with him. Barry thanks the hiring manager for working with him on these items and shares that he is hopeful that they can work something out. Barry says that he looks forward to hearing back from the hiring manager.

EQ EXERCISE: PLAN FOR NEGOTIATIONS

In order to negotiate successfully, you need to have a plan. Answer the following questions before you head to the negotiating table:

1. Job offer negotiations are stressful, but it's a good kind of stress to have. After all, the job offer is what you have been working for! How will you manage your feelings of stress to be effective?

   _____

   _____

2. You need to be realistic about what you are asking for. What can you reasonably ask for? How do you know that what you're asking for is reasonable?

   _____

   _____

3. You need to approach the negotiation with empathy by understanding the employer's point of view. What do you know about the employer's perspective?

   _____

   _____

4. To make the negotiation work for both sides, you need to be flexible, creative, and willing to collaborate. What alternatives can you suggest?

   _____

   _____

(continued)

(continued)

_____

_____

5. Use your self-awareness skills to determine what job aspects are most important to you and what terms you absolutely need to have in order to accept and be happy in the new job. What are your limits, the things you will not give up?

_____

_____

6. Think about which job aspects are least important. That is, what can you possibly live or start without? What terms of the job are you willing to be flexible about?

_____

_____

7. Think through the employer's possible objections to your requests. What are your responses to these objections? See the table for examples.

_____

_____

_____

_____

EMPLOYER COMMENT	YOUR EQ RESPONSE
"We have never paid a starting engineer that kind of salary."	"I can understand that. However, I do bring unique skills and expertise that I feel bring added benefit and value, which will increase your sales and profit and hopefully cover the amount I am asking for."

EMPLOYER COMMENT	YOUR EQ RESPONSE
	Can you consider this and possibly make an exception?"
"We have people with 10 years of experience not making that much."	"I understand that you want to be fair. However, in doing my research and networking, I know that the average salary rate for someone at my level in this industry is in line with what I am asking. I would like to work here, but I need to be fair to myself."
"Our company policy for new starts is two weeks."	"Have you made any exceptions with your new hires? I know with today's changing job market and the movement of employees between companies that many organizations are reconsidering their policies and bringing them in line with all the changes."

When you have a well-thought-out plan for a negotiation, a positive outcome is more likely. However, note that you are taking a risk when you choose to negotiate and your ongoing working relationship is impacted by how smoothly the negotiation goes.

Using Conflict Management and Negotiation to Choose a Career

Some careers require good conflict management and negotiation skills. For example, salespeople and lawyers obviously need to be comfortable in dealing with conflict and in negotiating deals. Purchasing agents and buyers also need to be skilled at conflict management and negotiation.

My husband and I worked with a real estate agent who was skilled in these areas. He guided us through the process of selling the home we had lived in for 10 years and buying a new one in a way that made us happy so that we would call on him for future transactions. He empathized when we experienced feelings of loss as we sold the home that held so many memories for us. He knew when to support and cooperate with us and when to challenge us to stretch and compromise in working out a deal that all parties could accept. He displayed his emotional intelligence by developing a good rapport with us and connecting with us in a way that showed us that he understood our needs. He communicated his understanding and always did what he said he was going to do, from making a phone call to getting information for us. His level of accountability made us trust him. He was good in keeping in constant contact with us and in listening. He was also assertive enough to give us feedback as needed. When he had to manage disagreements with us, he used his empathy, the solid working relationship that he built with us, and his sense of humor to ease the tension involved.

Using Conflict Management and Negotiation to Find the Right Job

Earlier I spoke of conflict management in the sense of dealing with conflict between two people. Now I want to focus on personal conflict, meaning conflict that arises within you as you go through the job search. On your journey to find the right job for you, you may face many problems. How you deal with these problems has a large impact on your success.

For example, you go down a path that leads you to a job that interests you. However, you find that you need to earn a particular certification to be eligible for the position. You also learn that there are no current openings in several companies that you targeted. You now have choices to make on how to deal with this new information. This new data conflicts with the direction you were heading. How do you resolve this conflict? Ignoring the information is not being honest with yourself and not using your self-awareness and social awareness. This can lead to a bad choice and further frustration trying to obtain a job that you are not currently qualified for, on top of such a job being difficult to find at this time. To be emotionally intelligent in this situation, use the information and manage your feelings to take effective action (self-management). For example, one route is to obtain a job that is more available, even though you are less interested in it, and then work to obtain the certification that is needed for the job you really want. At the same time, stay connected with people in the companies you targeted to find out when an opening becomes available. This strategy involves delaying gratification and requires self-control, self-discipline, motivation, adaptability, and optimism! These are all the self-management skills that you are now putting into action.

Using Conflict Management and Negotiation to Get the Job Offer

The purpose of the interview is to connect with the interviewer and influence him or her to see you as likeable. When conflict arises in an interview, the goal is to resolve it in a respectful but assertive way. You show respect by acknowledging other perspectives and by being polite, and you show assertiveness by confidently expressing your views. For example, what happens when you and the interviewer have different views on a way to approach a situation? Tension automatically arises, and you need to be aware of this and deal with it successfully in order to move forward in a positive way. If you choose not to express yourself or if you are too vague in your responses, the employer will not know what you are all about and might not consider you further. On the other hand, if you create more conflict by being unyielding, you may push away the potential employer.

Some interviewers create conflict on purpose because they want to test your conflict management and negotiation skills. The interviewer in such a case might be looking for a leader who is comfortable with conflict and who will challenge employees. How can you respond to such a situation in an EQ way? Stay calm. Use your self-talk to ask yourself, "What is this interviewer trying to do? How can I best respond?" You have to know yourself, manage your feelings in the moment, size up what the situation is calling for, and respond appropriately in order to perform your best in the situation.

An executive client once shared with me that he walked into a high-level interview and was told to sit in the red chair. But there was no red chair, just a blue one. The interviewer then went on to ask a series of antagonizing questions, and the client did his best to respond. The interview ended without any debriefing or discussion about what transpired. The client felt that he was no longer interested in the company if this type of interview was part of its tactics and culture. He realized, however, the value of emotional intelligence in being able to be in the moment and respond effectively. The more aware he was of his emotions and thoughts, the interviewer's emotions and actions, and the situation, the more choices he realized that he had on how best to respond.

Clients have asked me, "If you know that a company or interviewer is looking for a certain quality or trait, should you act like you have it, even if you don't?" Your lack of the trait could eventually hurt your success on the job if you are hired and it was a characteristic that the employer was actively seeking. However, if the employer is looking for a trait that you are not strong in, but are willing to develop, you can communicate this information to the employer and give an example of how you possess the quality and how you plan to continue developing it. In this way, you negotiate your status with the employer. You are saying you have some of the quality, but you are willing to acquire more of it if you are hired for the job.

Negotiation skills certainly come into play when you are offered a job. A job offer (which you should ask for in writing) describes the terms of the position, which includes information such as salary, benefits, weeks of vacation, and starting date. When you are offered a job, acknowledge the offer and thank the employer. You then need to decide whether you want to negotiate any of the terms of the offer or accept it outright. It is acceptable to ask the employer if you can have a couple days to review the offer and terms. You may want to have time to discuss the offer with your significant other, for example. However, you do not want to take so long that you risk the company rescinding the offer. Remember, it is your choice on whether to negotiate the terms of an offer. Only negotiate if you feel confident in your conflict management and negotiating skills. Use your EQ and also recognize that, for some positions, negotiating is not an option.

Influence: Using It in Networking, Interviewing, and Leading

In the earlier section in this chapter on honesty, integrity, and trust, I mentioned Doug Hall's marketing traits that I described as BCD for short: benefit, credibility, and difference. These traits apply not only to marketing situations, but also to anyone who wants to be able to influence and develop others and become a leader.

Influencing and developing people are complex social skills. They are at the top of the hierarchy of social skills and build on all the lower skills in the pyramid. (Refer back to Figure 6.1 at the beginning of this chapter.) Influence begins with the lowest skills in the social skills hierarchy: honesty, integrity, and trust (credibility in Hall's terminology). Leaders have to be able to gain the trust of their followers. They do this by displaying their integrity in the way they express their views and through their actions.

In order to influence people, you must be able to communicate a benefit to them. If your message is difficult to understand or your communication skills are weak, people will likely stop listening to you, and you will lose your influence.

People follow leaders whom they like and admire and who they believe will make a difference and have an impact. (This impact could be good or bad for society, depending on the beliefs of the leaders and the followers.) You will likely follow someone if you believe in that person's cause and if his or her interests are in line with yours.

The best leaders want their employees to succeed. Leaders understand that if their employees are happy and successful, then they will be productive and results will follow. This is where the skill of developing others comes into play. Leaders with EQ show through their interactions with employees that they value employees and their work. Such leaders use their skills of collaboration and conflict management to work with others, resolve differences, and support group goals.

EMOTIONAL INTELLIGENCE IN ACTION

Will's position as an executive in charge of managing and implementing quality control processes with a tool manufacturing company has been eliminated due to a large reorganization. Will is 61 years old and wants to continue working, but he is concerned about who is going to hire him at this point in his career. Through networking he has several discussions with executive staff at a company that is expanding into South America and needs someone to put quality control processes into action there.

Demonstrating his self-confidence, Will shares his experience and expertise and offers to map out a plan, which he later describes to the company executives and the board. They agree that he would be a huge benefit for their company, but they express concern about paying him what he wants and is worth. Will states that he is willing to work with a four-year contract, which gives him enough time to complete his plan while also establishing an employment end date and cap on his salary for the company. It is a win-win for both sides. Will has good self-awareness and social awareness and is able to manage himself in a way to use his social skills to convince the company and its decision makers that he is the person to hire.

EQ EXERCISE: BROADEN AND SHARPEN YOUR INFLUENCING SKILLS

In order to influence others and lead others, you need to know what you stand for and how you are going to communicate it. In preparation for your job search, your goal is to influence the interviewer as well as people whom you network with who might have a connection to a job lead or opportunity. Reflect on and answer these questions:

What unique qualities can you bring to the industry or organization?

_____

_____

What unique experience and education (formal, informal, on-the-job training and so on) do you have that employers would be interested in?

_____

_____

What are the employer's main needs and concerns?

_____

_____

How can you meet those needs and concerns? (Share skills and past accomplishments.)

_____

_____

What might be some obstacles to overcome on your end and on their end in order to get the job offer?

_____

_____

_____

What steps can you take to overcome these obstacles? Think creatively!

_____

_____

When will you take these steps? What exactly are you going to do and when?

_____

_____

Using Influence to Choose a Career

Influencing and developing skills are not needed in the process of making a career choice as much as they are when you are working in a career. Careers with a high amount of interaction with people, such as in selling, promoting, or teaching, require the skill sets of influencing and developing. Careers in human resources, public relations, ministry, and social work are other examples of occupations that require workers to have these higher-level social skills to be effective and successful. If your career path and long-term goals include being a manager in any occupation or business, you will need to influence and develop others in effective ways that bring business results.

Using Influence to Find the Right Job

It is common sense that people become friends with people they like. People also help people they like. In Chapter 1, I made a case that likeable people are often emotionally intelligent people. They have good personal and interpersonal skills. Growing your likeability factor expands your potential for making connections and thus making your network useful in finding the right job and getting to the people who make the hiring decisions.

Using Influence to Get the Job Offer

In an interview, you sell yourself and try to position yourself as having what the employer wants. Selling is influencing, persuading, and convincing others to believe what you believe. Your performance and presentation in the interview become a snapshot of the relationship skills that you bring to the position and company.

What strategies can you use to persuade the employer to hire you for the position? Here are a few guidelines:

- Display confidence and credibility by answering questions honestly.

- Communicate clearly and ask for clarification when you lack understanding.

- Send the message that you want to understand the employer's needs and assist the employer.

- Communicate the value and benefit that you bring and how you can make a difference in the company.

- Give examples of past accomplishments to persuade the employer that you can do the job because you have done similar projects in the past.

To get the job offer, you need self-awareness of what you offer, social awareness of what the employer needs, and self-management to present yourself and the information in a confident way so the employer can hear and be receptive to the message. You need to use your EQ!

Role Models with High Social Skills

Daniel Goleman says the best leaders are those who are high in emotional intelligence. They are often cognitively bright also, but their EQ truly shines and this is what draws others to like, follow, and emulate them. The role models I describe here who demonstrate highly developed social skills are all leaders in their fields.

Barack Obama, the 44th President of the United States, seems to be a truly emotionally intelligent leader in addition to being intelligent in a cognitive sense. The public views him as someone who is understanding and concerned. Coming from such a diverse background of races, religions, cultures, and geographic regions helps him to be empathic while having a broad sense of the reality at hand. He communicates eloquently and influences others with his strong beliefs and confidence.

Ronald Reagan, the 40th President of the United States, was a president who demonstrated high emotional intelligence as well. He had confidence and good awareness of his strengths and weaknesses and managed himself very well in the public eye. He had a good sense of humor that he used in tense situations, and he spoke genuinely. One of his major accomplishments was to negotiate a reduction in nuclear arms with President Gorbachev of the Soviet Union, which benefited both the USA and the USSR as well as the rest of the world.

One of my clients glowed with EQ. He was seeking a new executive position after he voluntarily took an early separation package from a Fortune 500 company in which he had worked for 20 years. Despite being unemployed, he showed confidence; his strong self-awareness and self-management skills were evident in how he answered questions and responded to others in the same situation. Working more than 40 hours a week, he conducted his job search with determination, yet he kept a sense of humor and optimism. He also used the outplacement services he had been given to their fullest degree. Most of his effort was directed to building a large social network. He did this by being genuine and sincere and reaching out to others. He communicated to others what kind of position he wanted, and he gave out information and contacts that were beneficial to others in return. Through gathering information from his network and his research, he came up with a list of companies to target that were a good match for his skill sets. He then worked hard to develop contacts in those places. He stretched himself to make cold calls when needed, which was not an easy task for him. As a result of his efforts, he landed a new position within three months of leaving his past position, which is a very short time for an executive-level job search.

Chapter Reflections

Chapter 1 defined emotional intelligence as combining your self-awareness and self-management with your social awareness and social skills for the purpose of creating an impact or outcome. Chapter 2 explained the building blocks of EQ and the process of reflecting on thought-feeling-behavior connections and using the information to manage yourself and others in the direction of your desired outcome.

In Chapters 3–5, you learned about three of the four skill sets of emotional intelligence: self-awareness, self-management, and social awareness. You have to develop a reasonable amount of all of these skills in order to be successful in the last set: social skills. Social skills include the ability to develop and maintain close relationships, to work well with others, and to lead others. These skills build on one other to form a hierarchy that ranges from simple trust and honesty to the highly complex skill of influencing and developing others.

As you might remember from the introduction, social skills are particularly important in stage IV (interviewing for a job) and stage V (negotiating and accepting a job offer) of the career transition process. H.I.T. is the foundation on which you will successfully build your career. Being honest with yourself when you choose a career or a particular job is starting off on the right track. During the interview, you want to show the interviewer that you are credible and trustworthy. Clear and assertive communication also is an important tool in conveying the benefit you can give to the employer, but remember to balance your assertiveness by also displaying a cooperative and collaborative spirit. You can use the higher-level influencing skills in the interview to persuade and convince the interviewer that you are the best person for the job. When you get a job offer, it's helpful to have conflict management and negotiation skills to negotiate the terms you want. Chapter 7 provides even more in-depth information on how to use your EQ during an interview.

PART III

Developing Your Emotional Intelligence to Achieve Your Career Goals

Part III focuses on how you can use your EQ skills in specific career situations:

- Chapter 7, "EQ Answers to Interview Questions: Impress Employers and Get the Job," focuses on how to show off your EQ to make the connection with the interviewer and further your advantage in getting the job offer.

- Chapter 8, "Job Search Obstacles: Overcome Them with EQ," points out the typical job search obstacles that interfere in the career transition process, as well as strategies and exercises to overcome them.

- Chapter 9, "EQ and Your New Job: Use It or Lose It," reviews each of the emotional intelligence skills in relation to their importance for ongoing career success. Examples and exercises are given that can help you use your developed EQ skills to achieve success in your new job. If you do not continue using the skills that you have developed in your job search, you will lose them. Using your EQ in your new job will continue to give you the advantage in performing at your best, thus giving you the edge in times of reorganization.

EQ Answers to Interview Questions: Impress Employers and Get the Job

Emotional intelligence continues to pick up momentum in the world of business and academia. More and more research supports the concept that emotionally intelligent employees, managers, leaders, and companies produce noticeable business results. Employers are now looking for EQ in their potential employees and leaders and utilizing assessments and directed interviews to assess a potential hire's emotional intelligence skills. Would you be ready to interview with just such an organization?

Preparation for the interview is the most important thing you can do to increase your chances of a successful performance. Behind every question is a need, a concern, or a targeted characteristic or quality that the interviewer is looking for you to address. You want to know what interviewers are looking for and then structure your answer accordingly and communicate it clearly. You don't have to memorize answers, but you want to be clear about the message that you give to employers when they ask you a particular question. I suggest writing an outline of your answer to common questions ahead of time as a way to prepare. Another way to prepare for an interview is to review your past accomplishments. Interviewers will ask you questions with regard to the items that you have listed on your resume, and you need to be able to share the accomplishment showing the skills and value you have brought in your past positions and now potentially what you can bring to their companies.

The goal of this chapter is to prepare you for the interview by helping you identify what EQ skills interviewers are looking for and to heighten your awareness of how they look for EQ in your performance. I will begin with the purpose of the interview and review important interviewing strategies that I have presented in earlier chapters. I will then focus on the content of quality answers to typical interview questions, as well as prepare you for those not-so-typical behavior-based questions that are asked in the interview to assess your personal and social skills.

Purpose of the Interview

Interviewers structure and direct interviews with a potential hire with the following goals in mind:

- To meet the individual
- To assess the candidate
- To gather data
- To find out important or missing information

Through the process of the interview, you have smaller goals to accomplish that relate to these interviewer goals (see Table 7.1). The ultimate goal for interviewers is to make a good decision about whether to hire a particular candidate for the position. Of course, your ultimate goal in an interview is to be the selected candidate and to get the job offer.

TABLE 7.1. INTERVIEW GOALS

Goals of the Interview	For the Interviewer	For You
Meet the individual.	Get to know you, the person.	Make a connection; come across as likeable; show your credibility.
Assess the candidate.	Evaluate the value and benefits that you can bring to the position and company; determine whether you can do the job and do it well.	Show that you will add value to the organization and describe the benefits that you can offer by communicating your accomplishments, experience, education, training, verbal skills, EQ skills, and leadership skills.

Goals of the Interview	For the Interviewer	For You
Gather data.	Ask questions to obtain the information needed to make a good decision. Observe your communication and other EQ skills in action.	Show your communication and emotional intelligence skills by displaying them in the interview.
Find out important or missing information.	Uncover any important information not covered by your resume.	Be aware of areas that the interviewer might want to address. If you are aware of points of concern, prepare to talk about them.

EQ Techniques for the Interview

You might have the skills and experience needed for the job, but unless you communicate this clearly in the interview, you will not get the offer. In order to interview well, you need to connect with the interviewer and sell yourself as having the necessary skills and expertise. These techniques will help you do just that:

- **Focus on three main points.** An attendee of a training session I facilitated told me that he has learned from giving presentations that an audience's attention span can hold on to only three main points. An interviewer has about the same attention span, so pick three points or messages that should be highlighted throughout your overall interview performance. Plan how you will get your points across through your answers to interview questions. For example, if you wanted to emphasize your extensive research and contributions in the health-care industry, you could talk about it as a key accomplishment when the interviewer asks what accomplishment you are most proud of.

- **Research what the company needs and share how you meet those needs.** Employers admire job candidates who show a real interest in their company by being knowledgeable and informed about their business. To sell yourself in an interview, you need to communicate the value and benefit that you bring. If you know what a company's needs are, you can share how you can meet those needs, which ultimately leads to business results. For example, if you learned that the company that you have an interview with is expanding its business internationally, you can share your knowledge of the targeted countries and your fluency in the languages of those regions, which can make you an asset to the company in this expansion.

- **Know your brand.** Today's job market is very competitive, so setting yourself apart from the other candidates is very important. You distinguish yourself from others by branding yourself and showing what makes you unique or different. Branding is as critical in marketing yourself effectively as it is in marketing products. How do you want others to think of you and remember you when you leave the interview? If you brand yourself as the person who "goes the extra mile," how can you say this in the interview? Will it come across in your answers or the examples that you plan to share?

- **Create a good communication flow**. When two people are engaging each other and connecting in some degree, energy flows back and forth between them like the rhythm of a good tennis match. Richard Nelson Bolles (in his book *What Color Is Your Parachute?*) calls this kind of interaction the 50/50 rule of communication, in which each person in the conversation speaks and listens 50 percent of the time. You should strive for this type of communication in all of your job search–related meetings, especially interviews.

To get this 50/50 communication flow in an interview, keep your answers to questions short, clear, and to the point. Let the interviewer ask for more detail about any of the information that you share. When you do not fully understand a question (or a response), ask the interviewer for clarification. For example, you might say, "If I heard you correctly, you are saying that… ." You want to leave the interview with accurate information, and asking questions for clarification shows good listening and communication skills. Throughout the interview, look for a good time to ask your questions about what you need or want to know. Work them into the flow of the interview based on the topic you are discussing. After all, you are trying to decide whether this job is the right one for you.

- **Smile and show a sense of humor.** Have you ever noticed that it is hard to develop a connection with someone who does not smile or laugh? Smiles engage people. Even if you feel that you do not have much of a sense of humor, you can smile and laugh when the interviewer shows his or her sense of humor. Do a practice interview with friends or family members and ask them if they see you smile once in awhile.

Close an interview with three steps:

1. Ask for a business card so that you can write a thank-you note to the interviewer and have his or her contact information to follow up if needed in a week or two. In your thank-you note, highlight your interest in the job and the value and benefit that you can bring to the company. Keep it brief and to the point!

2. Make sure you ask about what the next steps in the selection process are and when you might hear back from the interviewer about consideration for the next round of interviews or a decision about the job.

3. Thank the interviewer for his or her time and consideration.

Quality Answers to Typical Questions

Before you answer a job interview question, ask yourself what the interviewer is looking for by asking this question. What information does he want to know and what skills is he looking for? How can you best respond to the question in a way that shows you can meet the organization's needs and have the necessary skills?

As I said at the beginning of this chapter, thinking about your answers before the interview is the best way to prepare for it. Because you are trying to make the biggest positive impact, decide what you may want to downplay in the interview and keep it out of your answers. Know how you will handle any areas of concern about your background in the interview.

To help you to prepare for interviews, this section reviews typical questions and provides directions and ideas on how to answer them in a way that demonstrates your EQ skills. With all interview questions, remember keep your answers brief.

"Tell Me About Yourself."

This open-ended question is often the first one asked. It is an introduction, and it sets the pace of the interview. Therefore, it is a very important question. Your answer will give the interviewer much information to explore.

So what do you want the interviewer to know about you? This may be a good time to introduce the three points that you want to carry through your interview. What professional experience do you want to highlight? You can talk about your past two job positions and the significant accomplishments you achieved in each of them. You can include two or three adjectives that describe you, which will help to brand you and allow the interviewer to remember you. Think of the skill sets you want to mention as you describe your accomplishments.

Clients often ask me if they should share personal information when they are asked this question, such as "I have been married for 20 years and have two children in college." My advice is to keep your response focused on your career, not your personal life. If you don't, you run the risk of sharing something that might work against you instead of for you. If an interviewer does casually ask some family and personal questions, it is up to you to decide how much you share. You can use such questions as an opportunity to develop stronger connections by sharing this information, but be selective. For example, if you are a fan of the same football team that the interviewer is (as evidenced by all the Pittsburgh Steelers paraphernalia in his office), this would be an excellent interest to share. Doing so starts an automatic connection and probably increases your likeability.

The focus of this question is on your self-awareness and self-management skills. You can communicate these skills in your answer by showing that you know your strengths and that you have maneuvered well from one position to the next.

Example of a quality answer:

> *My background is in marketing, and my key strengths are motivating and leading others as well as demonstrating innovation and creativity. For both of the Fortune 500 companies that I have worked for, I was responsible for leading the marketing efforts for the two top-selling brands. In my most recent position, I was instrumental in growing the market share for both brands by successfully managing teams to identify needs, create and implement ideas, and collaborate to make the needed changes in packaging and sales of these products. As a result, we were able to double our expected sales goals. I am now looking for an opportunity in another executive-level marketing position, such as this one, where I can deliver similar results.*

"Why Do You Want to Work for Our Company?"

The focus of this question is on your social awareness (how much you have learned about the company) and self-awareness (what you think you can contribute to the company). This is one of those questions where preparation is paramount. Before you show up for the interview, you need to research the company through its Web site; read newspaper articles, trade journals, and magazines; and talk with current or past employees. During your research, make notes about how your skills and experience would match the company's needs. Think about how you can contribute to the business and the value and benefit you can add.

Example of a quality answer:

> Your company has always been perceived as being the best in the industry. Not only are you profitable, but you also continue to grow in innovative areas. I read in the Business Courier about your expansion into the health-care industry. That sounds exciting and is very much in line with my interests and background. I have not only worked for several years in the health-care industry, but I also have stayed in touch with my colleagues in that industry. I have some understanding of the challenges that they face and have provided some good ideas to help them position themselves better in the market. I would like to do that for your business as well.

If you aren't asked this question, show your interest in the company by asking questions about the company or industry during the interview.

"Tell Me About One of Your Accomplishments at Company ABC."

This question focuses on your self-awareness and self-management skills. To answer it, first choose an accomplishment that is relevant to the position for which you are interviewing. The interviewer is looking for information on what you can do for his or her company. When you share your accomplishment story, talk about problems you faced and the actions you took to correct the problems, as well as about the results or goals you achieved. Mention the skills that you used and include your branding adjectives. When you describe yourself, think about how you want to sell yourself and what you want the interviewer to remember about you.

Example of a quality answer:

One of my biggest accomplishments at Company ABC is when I doubled the revenue of the small business from $125 million to $250 million in 12 months by building warranty support into one of the higher premium services offerings. I did this through conducting careful financial and market analysis as well through motivating and influencing my teams to sell this package. Shortly after that, I was promoted to district manager to solve similar challenges on a larger scale. My skills of planning, analysis, and marketing—along with my motivational and leadership skills— drove my success.

"Name Two Strengths and Two Weaknesses."

The focus of this request is to evaluate your self-awareness and your self-management skills. The key here is to pick strengths that are valued in the position you are interviewing for. Communicate each strength by giving an example of how you show it. Telling a short story will give the interviewer more data and richer detail about you and how you work.

Example of a quality answer:

One of my strengths is that I am very accommodating and accepting of others and their views. This strength helps me be a good team member and an effective leader. When I lead team meetings, I create an atmosphere of collaboration by showing that I value team members and by encouraging them to share their ideas openly and respectfully. Team members have told me that they appreciate my approach because they feel comfortable expressing their ideas. As a result, the team engages in a rich and thoughtful discussion during meetings. This type of discussion has lead to some pretty creative and diverse ideas that have been put into action and have had a positive effect on the company's sales.

With regard to choosing a weakness, pick an overused strength rather than a true weakness. In this way, you are still presenting yourself in a positive light while being honest about your flaws. For example, if one of your strengths is self-discipline, you are skilled at setting a plan and carrying it through. This strength has served you well in most situations, but you are also aware that sometimes you need to be flexible and open to change. Give an example of how you are aware of this weakness, and then explain how you manage it or are working to improve.

Example of a quality answer:

One of my weaknesses is flexibility. I am very self-disciplined and good at setting a plan and carrying it through. Although this trait has served me well in reaching my goals, I have learned that sometimes I need to balance this determination with flexibility and openness to doing things differently. For example, in my last position, I would save my administrative tasks for Fridays, which allowed me to be more focused on delivery of services during the week. Yet I began to dread Fridays because that's when I had to do the mundane administrative work. My supervisor suggested that I spend an hour at the end of each day on administrative tasks instead, thus freeing up Fridays for enjoyable activities and balancing my duties better. Knowing that I need to be more flexible at times, I pushed myself to try out her suggestion. The first couple of weeks were difficult, but I eventually embraced this new way of doing things, and then I was back to looking forward to Fridays, like most people!

"How Would Others Describe You?"

The focus of this question is on your social awareness and social skills. Basically, the interviewer wants to know how you get along with others. The "others" in your answer can be your last manager, your direct reports, and your coworkers. You should be ready to answer on behalf of all of them. The answer you give should show your willingness to collaborate, compromise, and communicate.

The interviewer wants to know whether you will fit into the team, department, or company. Your answer to this question will help him make this determination. The interviewer will also consider your gender, race, ethnicity, appearance, age, experience, and education. At this point, you only have control over what you say and how you say it; you can't change these other factors. Displaying your emotional intelligence may outweigh or offset any of the factors that you think might work against you in the situation.

When you describe how others see you, give an example that shows the trait you are describing. An example enriches your answer and gives the interviewer more information about you.

Example of a quality answer:

My manager would describe me as very dependable and committed. For example, because I live near the office, I have come in early on bad weather days to open it and greet any clients who have also made it in to our center despite the inclement weather. Many of the staff cannot make it on time because they live a distance away. In these situations, I want our clients to know we are here to serve them and that they can count on us.

"Why Should I Hire You?"

The focus of this question is your self-awareness and self-management skills. The interviewer wants to gain information to help him rule you in or rule you out. He has a tough job, and this question helps him with a process of elimination. The interviewer wants to know if you, compared to the other candidates, will be the one to work harder; work more efficiently; be more productive, dependable, and committed; and deliver the results that he needs and is looking for. This is not the time to be humble or modest. Speak up and brag a little bit. Tell him what you can offer.

Think of your competitors and the abilities or traits that you have that those others might not. Emphasize your three key points and use your branding adjectives. This is the time when your competitiveness needs to come out. Look at the job interview as a contest. The reality is that there is only one winner and many losers.

Example of a quality answer:

> *I know I can do the job and do it very well. I shared my accomplishments as marketing director at Company X with you, and I feel that I can achieve these same results within your organization. I bring with me many contacts in the field, and I will utilize these connections in this position to expand the company network. I know that my fluency in Spanish would be an asset in working with your Latin American customers, and I already know several members of your executive team from my involvement with them in the Chamber of Commerce. I feel that I have a good working relationship with them even before I begin.*

"What Salary Are You Expecting for This Position?"

The focus for this question is your social awareness and social skills. Companies want to know whether they can afford you. Many sources state that whoever throws out the first number is at a disadvantage. If you throw out a number too low or in the exact range, you cut down your potential earning power because the employer will offer you that amount. If you throw out too high a number, employers might not consider you further because you are out of their league, so to speak. The recommendation is that you let the interviewer give you the first number, but this recommendation can be tricky to follow. If an interviewer pushes you to give a number first, give a range. (Do some Internet searching on sites such as www. salary.com or www.salaryexpert.com to find ranges of salaries for like positions before the interview.)

One way to get out of answering this question is to ask the interviewer what the range is for the position. Another way is to let the interviewer know you would like to understand the responsibilities of the position in greater detail before you can discuss salary. What is important is how you approach the topic. You want to show confidence and trust that together you can work out this detail. You also need to read the interviewer's reactions and respond accordingly. If he pushes to know, give a salary range. Do not be unyielding.

Example of a quality answer:

This position is similar to my last job, but it is in a different industry and with a larger company, so I am not sure what range to expect. Can you tell me the range that you are considering for this position, and then we can work from that?

EMOTIONAL INTELLIGENCE IN ACTION

Katie is interviewing for a sales executive position. She has prepared some answers to common interview questions and researched the company through the Internet, as well as talked to a neighbor who used to work at the company. Katie knows what she can offer the company in the way of skills and experience and also knows the salary range that she can expect. In the interview, she is able to communicate her answers clearly due to her preparation.

When the interviewer asks her about salary expectations, she says she is flexible and asks what range is being offered for this position. The quoted range is much lower than she expects. She asserts herself and says that she is disappointed to hear the low salary amount and that her research has led her to expect the range to be much higher. She communicates openly and genuinely and speaks up and expresses herself. She wants a larger salary and has the social awareness to know that this goal is realistic, given her skills and experience. She manages herself well in how she presents her case to the employer and speaks up in a confident and respectful manner. She uses her EQ to influence the employer to consider a higher salary, and it works! The interviewer comes back with a higher salary offer.

"What Are Your Professional Goals, and How Would They Fit into This Position and Company?"

The focus of this question is on your self-awareness and social awareness. Business is run by goals and targets. You need to know what the company goals are and how you fit into the picture. The employer wants to know that you are goal-oriented and that you have your own personal and professional goals that you have achieved, because past achievement and success predicts future achievement and success.

Research has supported the idea that when an employee's goals are in line with an employer's goals, both parties benefit. If you know that your goals are in line with the company's goals and can communicate this fit, you can make the interviewer feel more confident that you are the right person for the position and company.

Example of a quality answer:

> My goal is to bring my current expertise and experience to this position to serve customers, thus producing similar sales results as I have achieved in the past. However, I like to be challenged and continue to grow my skills, so I am looking forward to transitioning into this industry and to taking on more responsibilities as I learn and contribute to the business. Your company values, "To serve others with respect and integrity...," which I saw on your Web site, are very much in line with my core values. I believe you must always put respect and integrity first and foremost, especially with the customers whom you serve.

"Why Did You Leave Your Last Position?"

This question is asked to assess the reasons for leaving a job and focuses on self-management, social awareness, and social skills. It provides useful information about how you have maneuvered in the world of work or in your career.

Today, unlike 20 years ago, there are fewer stigmas around losing your job, because most companies have had to restructure and make changes to adjust to the failing economy, and this restructuring has entailed layoffs. Interviewers want to assess whether you left your previous jobs of your own accord or were let go by the prior company. If you were let go, they want to know whether it was due to a personal issue or if you were part of a bigger restructuring or reorganization that affected many people and not just you. No matter what your situation is, always be honest.

Whatever your situation, you certainly will have many emotions concerning your past job loss or current unemployment. It is best to vent and talk about these feelings with family and friends so that you don't dwell on negative emotions or on a negative view of your last company when you are out networking and interviewing. This negativity will push others away. Again, use your EQ and stay aware of your feelings and thoughts and manage them so they do not get in the way.

If you were fired from a job due to your performance, you will have difficulty with this question. You have to be honest, but try to spin it in the most positive way for you. Emphasize the fact that you have learned from the experience, made some positive changes, and are ready to move on. Blaming others or your boss in this case would not be emotionally intelligent and would work against you. A career coach can help you develop an answer to this question that is honest and pertains to your unique situation.

If you have left the position because you did not like your work, let the employer know what you didn't like, what you did enjoy, and what you are now looking for in your next job. If you left because you did not get along with your boss, this is a big opportunity to use your EQ skills! Be honest. State there was a conflict between you and your boss. How you describe the situation will make the difference in how the interviewer perceives you. Do not come across as bitter. Describe how you managed yourself by focusing on resolving problems and overcoming disagreements and conflicts. Use your EQ and stay objective and do not belittle or discredit your former boss. Doing this gives the interviewer a sense of what you may be like in working for him.

Example of a quality answer:

I have a fairly easygoing nature and get along with almost everyone I have worked with. However, in my last position, I had some conflict with my supervisor. She was new to the company and was hired to deliver some big changes to boost sales. I was in support of the changes, but I disagreed with her style and how she went about implementing the changes. She did not take time to understand the current status of operations. She had an overbearing and abrasive style and would criticize employees in front of other employees when they did not comply quickly enough or well enough to meet her standards. I do not work well under this style of leadership. I work best with managers who recognize their employees' strengths and give them the freedom to do the work in their own way, but also give feedback in a supportive way on areas where they need to grow. I did my best to manage my emotions on the job and decided, after reviewing the political climate, that it was best to go along rather than assert my view when I interacted with her. This situation is one of the reasons that led me to look for another position.

Another example of a quality answer:

I value honesty first and foremost, and my last boss was not honest. I witnessed his dishonesty firsthand in his interactions with others, and it led me to wonder whether he was being honest with me. It was hard for me to work with him and for him based on my lack of trust in him and the fact that I did not respect him due to his lack of integrity and credibility. I am thus looking for a company with honest management that follows the same core values as I do.

"What Is Your Leadership Style?/What Kind of Leadership Style Do You Work Best Under?"

The focus in these questions is on all four areas of EQ: self-awareness, self-management, social awareness, and social skills. If you are interviewing for a leadership role, know your management style and what it says about the kind of person you are. Know how you impact, influence, and lead others. Have an example ready that shows all of your major skills.

Example of a quality answer:

I lead by example as well as provide the structure and direction for my staff. I develop and communicate clear expectations of them and work to keep open lines of communication through one-on-one meetings, both formal and informal. I reflect on the strengths of my staff and utilize their strengths in targeting our goals. My style has worked very well in that my teams usually exceed their goals and objectives. My staff retention and satisfaction are also high. Staff often stay for long periods of time in my department and tell me that I am approachable and concerned, but that I am also firm in staying the course with regard to mission and priorities.

For example, about a year ago, I had to implement a change in our documenting system, and this change was met with much initial resistance from my staff. To deal with this challenge, I had someone from our partner company come and talk to the employees about their experiences with this new system. This discussion helped to set the seed of change, and I encouraged staff to think about how we could best implement this system. The person I chose to come and talk to the group was great because he had a good sense of humor and a different perspective, which was well received by my staff.

If you are not interviewing for a leadership role, be prepared to answer the question on the kinds of managers whom you work well under. Your answer to this question shows your awareness of different styles, as well as how you work in relation to authority.

Example of a quality answer:

The kind of management style I work best under is someone who defines my job clearly and then lets me do it. I do not work well with managers who need constant feedback and interaction. I need to know they have enough trust in my ability to do the job and do it well. I am fairly independent. I keep communication open by e-mail and checking in on a weekly basis by phone or in person. I like knowing what the rules and expectations are and then having some flexibility to accomplish the tasks.

For example, my boss at Company XYZ set the parameters that I needed to work within and then allowed me the flexibility and creativity to achieve the targeted goals. Together we set the goal of improving the company's image in the community. I was able to explore many ideas and kept my boss informed. The result was that I developed and implemented a very successful co-op program as well as a scholarship program with the local community college, which improved the organization's image and community relationships, as well as enhanced the caliber of our staff.

EQ Responses to Behavior-Based Questions

Interviewers can assess your EQ by asking behavior-based questions. In these questions, interviewers ask about ways that you have handled issues and problems in the past. By tapping into your past behaviors, they hope to learn how you will approach similar situations in the future. They determine whether you have the skills they are looking for by evaluating the examples you provide.

In the book *The EQ Interview,* author Adele Lynn shares 250 behavior-based questions that interviewers can use to assess emotional intelligence competencies. She has done a thorough review, but I think it would be laborious for you as a job seeker to plan and prepare answers to 250 questions! Instead, I recommend preparing answers to the 10 target areas from which many EQ interview questions stem and then gathering your thoughts, ideas, and examples of how you show your emotional intelligence. If you know how to handle these 10 areas, you will be prepared to deliver a good answer with a good example no matter what particular question is asked. I describe each of these areas in the following sections.

Emotion Identification and Expression

With questions about emotion identification and expression, the interviewer is assessing your self-awareness, in particular your awareness of your feelings and mood in the workplace. The interviewer wants to understand how in touch you are with your emotions and how you manage them day to day. The interviewer wants to know if you are aware of the triggers that can set you off and how you deal with them.

The following are examples of questions that target this area. Consider them as you prepare your interview responses:

- Think of times when you were angry at work. What was the situation and how did you handle it?

- Think of a time you were frustrated because a project was not going well. How did you cope with the situation? What action did you take?

- Think of events or situations at work in which it is easy for you to get angry or frustrated. How do you manage these situations?

Awareness of Your Strengths, Weaknesses, Beliefs, and Values

Another aspect of self-awareness that the interviewer wants to assess is how well you know your strengths and weaknesses and how they impact your work performance and relationships. The interviewer also wants to assess your understanding of what you need from a job and how you deal with situations in which your beliefs are challenged. Here is an example of this type of question: Think of a time when the company that you worked for did not act in line with your values; how did you deal with it?

Goal Orientation

Goal orientation relates to self-management skills. With goal orientation questions, the interviewer wants to assess your overall belief that you can do the job and can achieve the goals established by the company. The interviewer wants to know how you direct and drive your behavior and how successful you have been. Here are some examples:

- Think of a time when you had some strong doubts about achieving success on a project. How did you manage these doubts and what was the outcome?

- Think of an example of a goal that you set and achieved. What was the situation and what actions did you take? What were the obstacles that you faced?

- Think of a time when you did not accomplish what you set out to do. What happened? What lesson did you learn?

- What motivates you to achieve your goals? What motivates you to meet or surpass the expectations of the company and others?

Response to Feedback and Dealing with Failure

The interviewer assesses your self-management and social skills by evaluating how open you are to feedback from your manager and others. The interviewer also wants to know how you deal with mistakes and failure. The interviewer is looking for your ability to be honest with yourself and others. The interviewer can gauge your attitude and how optimistic you are from your answers to questions such as the following:

- Think about a time when you made a mistake. How did you deal with it? What happened, and what was the impact?

- Think of a time when your manager shared feedback about your performance that you did not agree with. How did you respond?

- Think of a time in which you felt like giving up on a project or assignment. What was the situation, and how did you handle it?

Stress Management

With stress management questions, the interviewer is evaluating your self-awareness of stress in your daily work and your self-management skills in how you handle it. The interviewer also is discovering how you control strong emotions when under stress with questions such as the following:

- Think of a time in which you were stressed at work. What was the situation, and how did you handle it?

- Think of a time in which you said or did something at work that was not typical behavior of you that indicated you were under stress. For example, you might have lost your temper or said something that you later regretted. How did you become aware that you were stressed? Did you take any further action?

Adaptability and Creativity

To further assess your self-management skills, the interviewer asks questions about how you deal with change and how adaptable you can be. The interviewer looks for good problem-solving skills, creativity, and possibly innovation. The interviewer may want to know wheter you are a cautious person or willing to take risks, and the kind of position that you are interviewing for will be a factor in which quality the interviewer is looking for. For example, in a leadership position, risk taking is valued. The following questions are geared toward assessing your adaptability, creativity, and risk taking:

- Think of how you handled a change in your past job. What was your attitude and approach to managing it?

- Think about a time in which you were creative or innovative. What was the situation or challenge, and what did you achieve as a result of your creativity or innovation?

- Think about a time at work that you took a risk or tried something new. How did it turn out? What did you learn from the experience? Did it affect your future risk taking?

Awareness and Management of Others' Emotions and Ideas

The interviewer is looking for your social awareness and social skills, in particular your ability to be empathic and see things from others' perspectives. The interviewer wants to assess how well you listen to and otherwise perceive others and their situation. The interviewer is also assessing your acceptance and management of individual differences. Here are some sample questions for this area:

- Think of examples in which you were aware of how others on your team were feeling. How did you respond to them? Did you validate their feelings? Were you supportive of them and the situation?

- Think of times in which your beliefs were very different from a coworker's, but you had to work together. How did you approach this person and how did you handle disagreements?

If you are interviewing for a leadership role, the interviewer might ask a question such as the following:

- How do you assess the mood of your team and manage and shape it? Think of a particular time when you did this. What was the impact on the team?

- Tell about a time when you were aware that your direct reports or team members were under great stress. How did you know? How did you handle them?

Managing Relationships/Teamwork

In evaluating your social skills, the interviewer is assessing your ability to develop and maintain relationships for work outcomes. With questions in this area, the interviewer is evaluating your communication and collaboration skills and looking for your ability to put company goals ahead of your own personal interests. Here are some sample questions:

- Think of a time in which you learned something from your coworkers that helped you in your job or career. How did it impact your relationships with them? Did you show appreciation or gratitude?

- Think of a time in which you helped a team member who was struggling with his or her work or job. What did you do to support him or her?

- Think of how you developed relationships in your past job positions. What actions did you take? Did you initiate or organize any activities to get to know others better?

- Think of the kind of communicator that you are. How do you keep the lines of communication open with coworkers, manager(s), and your direct reports? Think of one specific example.

- Think of a time you went beyond the expectations of your job to contribute to the workplace. What did you do, and what was the impact on others and the organization?

Awareness of Company Culture/Politics

As part of evaluating your social awareness and social skills, the interviewer wants to assess how clued in you are to the dynamics of an organization. To find out if you have an understanding of the company culture and whether you think you would fit in, the interviewer might ask questions such as the following:

- Think of a time in which you needed support to implement an idea. How did you go about gaining support? How did it turn out? Can you think of a time in which it didn't turn out the way you wanted it to?

- Think of a time when you did not connect with the decision makers and the impact that it had on your job. What was the lesson learned? Has it changed how you proceed in similar situations in the future?

- How do you influence the company culture and climate? Think of an example of your influence in this area from your past job positions.

Influencing and Leadership Style

Questions in this area mainly target the advanced social skills of leaders, which include managers to higher-level executive positions such as CEO. The interviewer is assessing your overall leadership style and your fit into the organization. The interviewer not only wants to know what your vision and ideas are for moving the business forward, but also how you will manage the organization and set the organizational climate to get there. By using questions in this area, the interviewer assesses your interest in developing others and your ability to influence others.

To answer these questions, think about your leadership style. There are many ways to describe your leadership style based on the number of leadership training models. Think of examples of how you have led your team to reach a goal or through a change or transition. Do you lead by example? Are you a hands-on manager? Do you lead by assessing the strengths of your staff and delegating responsibilities based on those strengths? Think of your personal and professional mission. Do they go together? How do you communicate your vision and mission to others?

If you are in a leadership role, think about how you create a positive workplace. What actions do you take? How do you motivate others to achieve? Think of an example of how you influenced and motivated a coworker or direct report to a higher level of functioning. What was the situation and the result?

Chapter Reflections

Because research has shown that emotionally intelligent employees, managers, and companies produce noticeable business results, employers are now looking for EQ in their potential employees and leaders. Employers utilize assessments and perform directed interviews where they tap into and assess a potential hire's emotional intelligence skills. You want to be prepared to answer these questions and give your best performance.

Preparation for the interview is the most important thing you can do to increase your chances of a successful performance. Write down an outline or key points you want to make for particular questions in advance, and know your past accomplishments and be able to communicate them clearly. Show what value and benefit you bring and how you can meet the organization's needs or solve its challenges.

Keep in mind that the interviewer has specific goals during the interview: to meet you, to assess you, to gather data about you, and to find out important or missing information about you. Your goal is to find out about the job and hopefully get the offer. If you are clear on these goals, you can help to achieve them for a win-win situation.

Interviewers can assess your EQ by asking behavior-based questions. These questions tap into your past job performance. Interviewers will ask about ways that you have handled issues and problems in the past to learn how you will approach similar situations in the future.

The interview is all about connecting with the interviewer. You make the connection by both the content of your answers and the way in which you interact with the interviewer. If you have worked to develop your EQ through the exercises in this book, your confidence will come across in the interview and in your interactions with others.

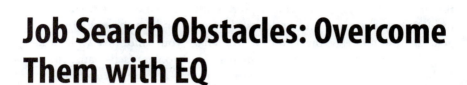

Job Search Obstacles: Overcome Them with EQ

Job search obstacles are anything that stands in the way of you landing the job that you want. They can include family, the job world, and anything that you do that hinders you from reaching your goal. This chapter will explain how to use emotional intelligence to overcome these obstacles. The process works through your thought-feeling-behavior connections. In this chapter, I will review common job search obstacles and suggest the particular EQ skills that are involved and how to use them to your advantage. This chapter also includes an exercise to help you assess your situation and a coaching model to assist you in overcoming obstacles.

Understanding the EQ Process of Overcoming Obstacles

Chapter 1 presented several definitions of emotional intelligence, and it was Reuven Bar-On's definition that addressed obstacles. He defines emotional intelligence as "an array of noncognitive capabilities, competencies, and skills that influence one's ability to succeed in coping with environmental demands and pressures." Obstacles are part of these "environmental demands and pressures." To succeed is to manage or overcome these obstacles and reach your goals.

IQ is important, but it is EQ that helps you use all your skills and attributes, including your IQ, most effectively, thus increasing your chance of success. You may have the cognitive smarts to understand that something is a problem, but unless you have the personal and social skills to do something about it, you will not be successful.

The emotional intelligence building blocks are the thought-feeling-behavior connections. You reflect on them, understand the connections, and make a conscious effort to change an area in support of the larger goal that you are trying to accomplish. You change your thought or behavior to manage your emotions and to move in the direction of your goal.

Self-awareness, self-management, social awareness, and social skills are involved in this process in some degree. With internal obstacles, you have to identify the obstacle and understand how it stands in the way of your goal (self-awareness). You then have to manage your emotions while dealing with stressors to take action to manage the problem (self-management). If the obstacle is external, dealing with it involves assessing people and/or the environment (social awareness) and then taking action to best manage others (social skills). (Remember the feedback loop that I introduced in Chapter 5?) You affect and are affected by others and use this information to guide you.

Conquering Common Job Search Obstacles with EQ Skills

Sorting out what you control and what you don't control is important when you face obstacles. Basically, you control you. You control your thoughts and behaviors, and you can manage your emotions. You control how you interact with others and how you respond to the environment around you. You do not have control over others or world events.

When you face a difficult situation, use your EQ to reflect on the reality of the situation by asking yourself these questions:

- What do I control?

- What can I do?

- What don't I control?

Obstacles that come from you can be changed by you. You are in the driver's seat. For example, if your current level of education is an obstacle in getting the job you want, you can go back to school to obtain the needed degree and remove it as a roadblock. Obstacles that arise from being part of a family or that come from the external environment can only be managed or influenced by you. For example, the current job market is very competitive. You cannot change that reality, but you can manage it by improving your networking skills by reading a book on the topic and attending a weekly networking group. You also can decide to do contract work for a friend to bring in some income, knowing that this job transition might take longer than planned due to the current economic situation.

Try these techniques when you face roadblocks in your job search:

- **Embrace obstacles and change.** Use your EQ skill of adaptability. Be aware of your thoughts and feelings and direct yourself. When faced with change, you sometimes might want to deny it or fight it. This is a normal reaction. Embracing the change, however, allows you to use your energy to deal with it rather than using your energy to avoid or fight it.

- **Stay positive.** Use your EQ skill of optimism. Remember from Chapter 2 that negative thoughts lead to negative feelings and thus impact your behavior in a negative way in the opposite direction of your goal.

- **Keep a sense of humor.** Use your EQ skill of emotional self-control. Avoid negative thoughts. Keep things in perspective, and don't take yourself too seriously. Don't try to do it all and do it perfectly.

- **Take care of yourself.** Use your EQ skill of stress management. You will be able to deal with stress and challenges more effectively if you are healthy. To maintain your health, see your doctors and dentist regularly, get plenty of sleep, watch your diet, exercise, and schedule fun activities with family and friends.

- **Develop what you lack.** Use your self-awareness and self-assessment skills to identify whatever it is that is keeping you from achieving your goal, and then work to develop that area. If you lack education, go back for more. If you lack experience, volunteer to get it. If you lack EQ, do the exercises in this book and grow your skills.

EMOTIONAL INTELLIGENCE IN ACTION

Rebecca left Company X, an international Fortune 500 company, choosing to take an early separation package that the company was offering to hundreds of employees in an effort to reduce costs. The company is well-respected and well-known, and the employees are viewed as top-notch professionals. Rebecca possesses many valuable skills: marketing, public relations, sales, and management. She is confident that other companies will be interested in her skills, but she is concerned that her lack of a college degree will be an obstacle. This concern is valid because many positions that match her skills ask for a bachelor's degree. She speaks with colleagues about her concerns, and the feedback she receives

(continued)

(continued)

is that the lack of a college degree might be an obstacle for some close-minded companies but that more companies will focus on her skill sets and the value she could add.

In her career coaching sessions with me, we explore how she can manage the issue of being screened out for interviews because of the lack of a college degree on her resume. First, she makes a choice to think positively and be optimistic that she will find an equally good position as the one she had left. Second, she decides to highlight her experience and skill sets in her cover letter and not mention her lack of a degree.

She also prepares a response for job interviewers when they ask about her lack of a college education: "I am aware that a bachelor's degree is one of the qualifications you listed, but I believe my extensive on-the-job training and experience through Company X enables me to bring a wealth of information and expertise to your company, particularly in the area of strategies to improve your productivity and profitability." If interviewers indicate that the degree is an important issue, she plans to add to her response, "I am certainly willing to work on a college degree on a part-time basis while employed with your company. It has been a goal of mine, but due to the long hours and high commitment at Company X, I had difficulty fitting it into my schedule. Company X did not see it as an obstacle."

In making this career transition, Rebecca displays high EQ. Her self-awareness is evident in her acknowledgment of her anxiety about finding a new job, her ability to verbalize her skills and accomplishments well, and her confidence that she can add value to a new employer. Her optimism and flexibility during the job search are proof of her self-management skills. Recognizing that her lack of education could be an obstacle and displaying empathy in addressing an interviewer's concerns show good social awareness. Lastly, she demonstrates her social skills in interviews by giving genuine answers and communicating her willingness to work to meet a new employer's requirements.

The following sections explain how you can use your emotional intelligence to address the obstacles you might face during the job search.

Family

Your unemployment not only affects you, it also affects your family. Although family members often mean well, they can be an obstacle during a job search. They want to support you, but their actions do not always turn out to be supportive. To help your family manage this transition, you will need to use a number of EQ skills:

- **Communication.** Discuss with your family what the days will look like in the months ahead. Suppose you plan to devote 40 to 50 hours a week to job hunting, but your spouse sees your unemployment as a time for you to work on the list of projects needing to be done around the house. This difference in expectations can be a huge obstacle and source of frustration on both sides if it is not discussed and worked out. Communicate your strategy and let your family know what is going on. If you are a young college graduate, let your parents know what your job search plan is and the steps you have already taken. They worry about you and seek reassurance that you are moving in a positive direction. This reassurance happens through communication. Communication is important in families and more so in times of stress and crisis when many people tend to withdraw.

- **Empathy.** Remember your family and significant others are affected by your job transition, too, and need your support and understanding. People respond to change and loss differently.

  If you have children, listen and respond to their concerns. When you consider your children's perspective, keep in mind that most children are egocentric. They think the world revolves around them. They do not wonder how unemployment is affecting you. (That concern comes later and is different based on the age and maturity of the children.) Instead, they worry about what will happen to them. So if Mom loses her job, a teenager might worry that Mom won't have money to buy her a prom dress. If Dad loses his job, children will wonder if they are still going on vacation. Most children and teenagers want to know whether they are going to have to move and change schools.

- **Optimism.** Be a role model for your family in how to deal with crisis and change. Your children will be in a job search one of these days and will remember how you handled it. They learn from your behavior whether or not you want them to, so it's best to model positive behavior. Children do not need to know all of your worries and fears. You can communicate the realities of the situation, but frame them in a way that is appropriate for your child to understand.

- **Cooperation, collaboration, and teamwork.** Let your family and significant other know that you want to work together to tackle the challenges ahead. Maybe you need to ask your daughter to drop her guitar lessons for awhile and your wife to cut her weekly manicures until you find a job. If you work together to find solutions to problems that arise, everyone will feel like they are managing the situation.

You can ask your children or teenagers to help out around the house or do a task for you to support you in your job search efforts. For example, if you have an important phone call about a possible job, ask your children to help you out by playing downstairs, by not interrupting you, or by letting the dog outside if he barks. Helping others is a way of managing the anxiety that comes from an event and exerting some control over a situation that seems entirely beyond your control.

- **Emotional self-control and stress management.** Deal with your stress positively. Emotions are contagious. For example, if you are feeling angry and acting out at home, everyone else in the family feels the tension and is prone to get angry or upset more quickly. The better you deal with the job transition, the better your family will deal with it.

- **Self-confidence.** If you have confidence in yourself, your family and significant other will have more confidence that you can and will find another job. Use the thought-feeling-behavior connections. You need to think and act in terms of *when* you find your next job and not *if* you find another job.

- **Conflict management.** Accept that there will be disagreements and work to resolve them. Rarely do conflicts just go away; avoiding them just causes them to snowball. It takes less energy to deal with a conflict when it first arises than it does after months of letting it build up. Dealing with disagreements openly can help everyone move in a positive direction. Know that you might not agree at the end of your discussion. In fact, you may have to come to an agreement to disagree with each other at some point.

- **Adaptability.** During times of stress, it is normal to resort back to old, established, comfortable ways of doing things, but stressful times are often when new ideas and strategies need to be tried. Encourage each other to be flexible. Taking some small risks by doing things differently can lead to improved situations. Yes, you might fail, but that is part of taking risks. Talk to your significant other about options, possibilities, and the pros and cons of each of them. For example, the nonworking spouse might need to go back to work for a period of time, or relocation might need to be considered.

Age

To fight age discrimination, the government passed the Age Discrimination in Employment Act of 1967 (ADEA), which makes it illegal for employers to discriminate against job applicants who are older than 40. However, my clients have shared their experiences of possible age discrimination in the workplace. How can you approach this concern?

Remember that positive thoughts lead to positive feelings lead to positive behaviors. Think positively, be optimistic, and show your energy and enthusiasm (often a sign of youthfulness).

A positive attitude is a good start in facing this obstacle, but next you want to assess how it could be an issue and decide how you will manage it in your job search. Develop a strategy to be proactive in breaking down the obstacle. Think about what being older and more experienced brings to the position or organization that you are targeting. Make a list of what you have that someone younger with less experience does not have. Plan how you will communicate this in your answers in the interview.

Use your EQ skill of flexibility and motivation. For example, should you consider a consulting role or adjunct teaching role instead of a similar position in another company? If you do target a similar position in another company, does it make sense for you to offer your services for a finite period of time, such as three to five years, to complete a stated project or goal? This arrangement could be a win-win for both sides. You want to work for a few more years, and the company wants your expertise, but it does not want to pay you the salary that you require for longer than it needs to.

Being younger can work against you also because sometimes younger workers are perceived as lacking experience or not being professional. If this is a concern for you, how can you manage it? Use your social awareness and dress to look professional. Use your self-management skills to tame your energy and communicate how you can get along with others of all ages. Have an example ready to share in the interview if you suspect it is a concern of the interviewer.

EMOTIONAL INTELLIGENCE IN ACTION

Sam is a middle-aged man and very personable, but he realizes that he is showing signs of aging and wants to be competitive in the job market. Even though he hopes his age will not work against him, he does not want to add any further

(continued)

(continued)

credence to this factor. So he steps back and takes a look at himself and how others may view him and decides to sharpen his image. He shaves off his facial hair, buys new glasses, and purchases a new shirt and suit to look polished and up-to-date. He is using his self-awareness and social awareness to make significant changes to advance his appearance, further his status, and bring him closer to attaining his targeted job. His skills shine better because his appearance no longer clouds his overall presentation.

Physical Handicap or Health Impairment

If you have a physical handicap, you will need to use your self-management skills of optimism, flexibility, and reality testing when you approach the job market. Use your self-awareness and social awareness to think of your job options. You have to be realistic in applying for jobs that you are able to do. Keep in mind your thought-feeling-behavior connection. If you think of your physical handicap as an obstacle, the interviewer will see it as an obstacle. If you show that you can maneuver well with your handicap and that it will not affect your job performance, then it will not be readily viewed as an obstacle.

When you have something less obvious, such as health impairment, you need to know how you can deal with this in your job and with your employer. For example, if you are diabetic, you might need to take two additional breaks during the day to check your blood sugar level and eat a snack. If you bring up this issue too early in the employment process, the employer may rule you out even though the health issue has no effect on your job performance. I think a good time to let the employer know about this issue is when you are offered the job. Then it can be a simple communication. Of course, you can show your flexibility and motivation by letting the employer know you will begin a half hour earlier or stay a half hour later to account for a full eight hours of work and reassure him or her that your health issue will have no impact on your job performance.

Managing Your Time

If you are currently unemployed, you will have time to devote to job searching, but you will also be in charge of managing that time. This is different than when you were working and you were told when you had to be at work and what tasks you needed to complete within a set time structure.

On the other hand, if you are still working while looking for a different job, you will have less time to use toward job searching and you will be challenged to use your limited time effectively. If managing time is a challenge for you, use your EQ skills:

- **Emotion identification and emotional self-control.** By dealing with your emotions effectively, you will spend less time worrying or obsessing about your situation and more time taking action steps. Are you thinking you have plenty of time to find a job? Or are you thinking there is not enough time to ever get things done? Look at your thoughts contributing to those feelings. Check out your thought-feeling-behavior connections.

- **Stress management.** If you deal with stress in a positive way, you will have more energy, and you will be more productive in the time that you have. When you deal with stress by exercising, talking to friends, or working on a hobby, you relieve stress and nurture your body. When you deal with stress in negative ways such as overeating, drinking alcohol, and sleeping excessively, you take more of a toll on your body, which can make you less productive.

- **Communication and assertiveness.** Work hard at your job search, but make sure you allow time to relax, take care of yourself, and enjoy your loved ones. If others want more of your time than you can give, use your EQ skills of assertiveness and communication to say no. Avoid overcommitting yourself. Keep in mind that taking care of yourself first can help you take better care of others in the long term.

- **Motivation.** Gauging your progress on a job search is difficult. One strategy is to establish long-term and short-term goals. Motivate yourself to stick to your goals and focus your efforts on them. Keeping a job search journal, as I mentioned in Chapter 3, can be very helpful in this area. If you list your goals and keep track of your progress, you have a record of your work and what you have accomplished. Don't forget to take time to reward yourself for your hard work!

Finances

When you are unemployed, you do not have control over the fact that you have no income, but you do have control over your current assets. When you are making decisions regarding finances, many of your EQ skills come into play:

- **Reality testing.** Assess your situation, taking into account your severance package and unemployment, and decide how many months you can job search before your savings are depleted. You can decide whether you need to take a part-time job while searching for a full-time one. You can decide what in your budget can be cut in order to pay the monthly bills and live sufficiently through this transition. It is a good time to speak with a financial consultant to understand your situation and determine best strategies.

  Research salary levels of various positions to increase your awareness and help you plan your job search strategy. Your finances will determine in part the type of job that you need to target. You are more likely to find a job doing the same kind of work in the same industry quicker than if you change careers or change to an entirely different industry.

- **Communication and teamwork.** Sit down with your spouse or significant other and have a discussion about budgeting and finances soon after you lose your job. You will need to decrease spending, and everyone in the family needs to be committed to this goal. It takes teamwork to keep the family budget on track. You also need to discuss what changes this career transition might bring, such as changing schedules or relocation.

- **Adaptability.** Look at your options and spend time considering each of them. You want your dream job, and hopefully you will get it. However, sometimes you to have a Plan A, Plan B, and Plan C. Plan A might be the ideal job. Plan B might be one that is more realistic based on your situation and the job market. Plan C might be a short-term solution while looking for a more permanent position, such as doing contract work or working temporary positions to bring in some income.

Economy

As I write this chapter, the United States has a struggling economy and is in a deep financial depression with a high unemployment rate. Because the number of job candidates competing for the same job is so large, it is a difficult time to be in the job market. So how do you proceed? With clarity, focus, and determination!

Although you have no control over the economy, you can manage yourself and your situation by using your EQ. Use your self-assessment skill to take a critical look at your skills and figure out where they fit best. There are still jobs to be filled, and there are still companies and industries that are growing despite the economy. Use your reality testing skill to target growing industries and companies instead of declining ones.

Use your EQ skills of motivation and optimism. If you find yourself focusing on how bad the economy is, stop your negative thoughts. Turn off the news. The reality is that it is a difficult time. Focus your energy and time on taking action toward your goal, and maintain an optimistic attitude that you will land a job soon.

Length of Hiring Process

Job seekers sometimes complain about the length of time it takes to land a job. In large companies, the whole hiring process from posting the position, to screening applicants, to conducting interviews, to extending a job offer can take many weeks. You have no control over this process, but you can influence the situation by following up if you have the name of a contact person. You want to be persistent and determined, but you do not want to be viewed as a pest.

If you get a letter stating the position has been filled, you can send another letter back thanking the employer for his or her consideration and asking him or her to keep you in mind should other positions become available. Show your interest in the company and attempt to strengthen the connection.

Technology Skills

Technology is growing fast. Requirements are constantly changing, and keeping up with the pace of progress is a challenge. But if you don't stay current in your technology skills, they will be an obstacle. You need to keep up with what is expected for the job that you are targeting. For example, if the positions you are applying for ask for a PMP (Project Management Professional) certification, then you will need it to stay competitive. Use your reality testing skill to determine what the expectations are.

Many people who find themselves in the job market for the first time in 10 years have to learn how to use the new technology, such as online networking and research tools, in order to be competitive. Learning these new skills takes motivation and adaptability. Resume writing has changed, and you will date yourself by doing a resume the way that you did it 10 to 15 years ago. Look at the newest resources on resume writing. Today you need to include keywords in your resume to accommodate electronic searches and to get your resume in the "to be called" pile. Keywords are those skills you have that the employer is looking for. For help in selecting keywords, look at the job postings that you are applying for and career resources that describe skills needed in various occupations, such as the *Occupational Outlook Handbook*.

EQ EXERCISE: ASSESS YOUR OBSTACLES

Rate yourself on each statement according to the following scale:

1 = True; 2 = Mostly true, but could improve; 3 = An area I need to work on

1. I know my strengths and how to use them in my job search.

   _____

2. I am aware of my weaknesses and how they affect my progress.

   _____

3. I know the kind of positions I am looking for. _____

4. I know the unique qualities I bring to employers. _____

5. I am very motivated, and it shows in my daily activities. _____

6. I am confident and determined that I will find the right job.

   _____

7. I check out my goals and plans with others and make changes when needed. _____

8. I have a well-written resume that captures employers' attention.

   _____

9. I am well prepared to interview for my targeted job position.

   _____

10. I have a job search plan that I follow and reevaluate from time to time. _____

11. I know the things that get in the way at home and deal with them effectively. _____

12. I keep my children and significant others involved and informed of my plans. _____

13. I have talked with my family about how to manage our financial situation. _____

14. I manage my time very well, and it shows. _____

15. I do not let the status of the economy or job market deter my efforts. _____

16. I am aware of the new technology involved in the job search today, and I am developing my skills in this area. _____

Look over your answers and write down a few of the obstacles that you rated as a 3. An exercise at the end of this chapter will help you consider action steps to overcome these obstacles.

1. _____

2. _____

3. _____

4. _____

5. _____

Using a Coaching Model

When you are faced with a challenge or obstacle, positive self-talk and a positive attitude will help. As I have emphasized, managing your emotions and stress is also important. These are all things that you can do for yourself. But being able to see the challenge objectively and realistically can be difficult to do on your own. Sometimes it is helpful to seek the advice of trusted colleagues and friends when you are faced with an obstacle, especially if what you have tried has not proven successful. These people can give you new and different ideas. A career coach is another option to help you in those situations when you feel you need assistance in achieving your goal.

Before seeking help, though, you will want to try all that you can to coach yourself through the obstacle and in the direction of your desired outcome or goal. Dr. Jeff Auerbach, founder and president of The College of Executive Coaching and author of *Personal and Executive Coaching,* developed the Auerbach GOOD™ Model of Coaching. He teaches this technique to professionals learning to coach clients. Basically his model is broken down as follows:

- **Goal:** You state what your goal is. The more specific and measurable the goal is, the easier it will be to define and to evaluate whether you have achieved it.

- **Options:** List all the options or ways that you can reach the goal. Include steps, both large and small ones.

- **Obstacles:** With each option, think what obstacles could get in the way of achieving your goal. The idea is to troubleshoot ahead of time the ways you can manage or work around them.

- **Do:** Decide on the actions that you will take to move forward and when you will take those actions.

Dr. Auerbach's model helps you to think ahead and prepare. It is future-focused. You can adapt this model to your job search goals and obstacles.

When you develop a goal, you might want to consider using the SMART strategy. This strategy comes from the arena of project and performance management. It is a mnemonic that stands for these values or keywords:

- **S**pecific

- **M**easurable

- **A**ttainable

- **R**elevant

- **T**ime-bound

When you make a goal specific, measurable, attainable, relevant, and time-bound, the belief is that the goal is easier to attain and progress toward the goal is easier to evaluate.

Evaluation is the last step in this process. You evaluate by reflecting on the progress you have made or the lack of progress, whichever is the case. In the coaching process, I reflect with my clients on how their action steps were carried out each week and whether they were successful. If the actions were successful, possibly those actions might be incorporated on a regular basis. If they were not successful, the focus is on what other action steps can be tried. Set a time for yourself when you will come back and review your progress.

EQ EXERCISE: MAKE AN ACTION PLAN

This exercise is meant to help you reflect on obstacles in your job search and to plan immediate actions that you can take to move forward. Go back to the previous self-assessment exercise and look at the list you made of statements in which you rated yourself a 3. Write them below and list the specific action steps you can take to move ahead, as well as a date and time when you will take each step (such as tomorrow, next Thursday).

Obstacle: _____

Direct action: _____

Date of action: _____

Obstacle: _____

Direct action: _____

Date of action: _____

Obstacle: _____

Direct action: _____

Date of action: _____

Obstacle: _____

Direct action: _____

Date of action: _____

Obstacle: _____

Direct action: _____

Date of action: _____

Chapter Reflections

Job search obstacles include anything that stands in the way of landing a job that you want. Obstacles include family, the job world, and your own limitations. You can use your EQ to help you succeed by recognizing and solving problems, assessing situations realistically, and choosing to be optimistic. When you are faced with a challenge or obstacle, positive self-talk and a positive attitude will help.

To use your emotional intelligence to overcome obstacles, focus on thought-feeling-behavior connections and make a change in one area, thus causing the other areas to move in the direction of the desired goal. Self-awareness, self-management, social awareness, and social skills are all involved in the process of facing obstacles to some degree. You first have to identify and understand the obstacle (self-awareness). You then have to manage your emotions while dealing with stressors to take action to manage the problem (self-management). If the obstacle is outside of yourself, dealing with it involves assessing people and/or the environment (social awareness) and taking action to best manage others (social skills).

You can coach yourself through obstacles using the Auerbach GOOD™ Model of Coaching or seek out a career coach when you are feeling stuck and could benefit from the help of a professional.

By using your EQ skills, hopefully you will land the right job sooner than later. Once you start your new job, you want to continue using your skills to adjust, adapt, and excel. The next chapter provides ideas and examples on how to apply your EQ skills for success in your new job.

CHAPTER 9

EQ and Your New Job: Use It or Lose It

Research shows that emotional intelligence skills are important to success on the job. Joshua Freedman and Todd Everett in their *White Paper on the Business Case for Emotional Intelligence* share many interesting studies. One study performed in 2006 at an international petroleum corporation showed how EQ distinguishes between high and low performers. The researchers investigated relationships between international business capability, expertise, cognitive attitude, and emotional competencies. Through interviews, surveys, and focus groups, participants identified factors that separated average from superior performers. EQ-related competencies were stated twice as often as IQ-related ones in distinguishing the superior performers.

The business world sometimes wants to dismiss the importance of your emotions. However, ignoring your emotions will work against you. Many emotions surface when you start a new job. Use your EQ and manage them; you will feel better and perform more effectively.

In this chapter, the emotional intelligence skills are reviewed with regard to their usefulness in your new job and career. In order to make these skills work for you, you will need to use them all the time. The more you use them, the more natural they become. I will give examples of these skills in action on the job, as well as some exercises you can use to continue developing your skills.

Self-Awareness and Career Success

As you remember from Chapter 3, self-awareness consists of the following skills:

- Emotion identification
- Accurate self-assessment
- Self-confidence

All of these skills will be useful on your new job.

Emotion Identification

The more faithfully you listen to the voice within you, the better you will hear what is sounding outside of you.

—*Dag Hammarskjöld*

Emotions signal important information. Identifying your emotions every day will help you develop your thought-feeling-behavior connections, those building blocks of emotional intelligence. Let your emotions be your guide in what is happening in the workplace.

Be aware of your emotions as you interact with others. Think about what you want to come out of the interaction or working relationship. Use your self-talk to ask yourself, "What thoughts are traveling through my mind? How are those thoughts affecting how I feel and behave? Are they realistic?"

Note that your emotional state will affect others' emotional states. If you are happy and positive, this feeling will affect others in a positive way. If you are angry, this tension will rub off onto others and will affect staff productivity and performance.

Every day, make yourself aware of your impact on others. How do others respond to you? This awareness gives you feedback on how you are perceived. You can then reflect on this information and decide whether you want to change your behavior to produce a different perception, one more in line with your long-term goals.

EMOTIONAL INTELLIGENCE IN ACTION

Daniela is a very good sales representative who usually exceeds her sales goals. She is able to turn on her charm in front of customers and make solid connections. However, when it comes to relationships with the staff, she is very different. She keeps to herself and does not engage others. Her job and her family keep her busy, so she does not make time for small talk. She is all about getting her job done and spending the rest of the time on her personal and family interests. The staff sees her as having a superior attitude, as if she does not have time for them. One day Daniela attends a business luncheon at the request of her manager, and through some joking, she is made aware of how the staff perceives her. Of course, she feels bad in hearing that she is seen as cold and impersonal. She does not want to be viewed this way, so she decides to interact more with staff by attending more informal lunches and stopping by offices to say hello.

Accurate Self-Assessment

Consciousness of our powers increases them.

—Vauvenargues

There is no job security today. You can do a great job and still be let go due to a company reorganization. When bosses have to make decisions about cuts, they will evaluate your performance, and you will want to be evaluated as a top performer so that you can keep the job you worked so hard to get. To be an effective performer, you have to continually assess what you are doing well and what you need to improve on.

One way to assess how you are doing is to ask for feedback. Sometimes you might get feedback on a blind spot. *Blind spots* are qualities that others see but that you are not aware of. They can be a quality, trait, attitude, or behavior. They also are obstacles that can prevent you from attaining your goals. By asking for feedback from others or listening when others make comments about your behavior, you can decrease your blind spots.

Make sure you ask for feedback from your supervisor. Push for 6- or 12-month performance reviews. Listen closely to the feedback. Take it in and assess the information and use what makes sense. If you disagree, get more feedback from others. Can you look at the issue from your boss's perspective and try to understand how he sees it differently than you?

The better you know yourself and your goals, the better able you are to make sound decisions about your career path. There might be opportunities to move up the management ladder. You will need to decide whether you want to advance or to stay where you are. So it is up to you to know your strengths, weaknesses, and career direction and make a proactive choice and decision that is the best for you.

EMOTIONAL INTELLIGENCE IN ACTION

Josh wants to rise up through the management ladder, but he continues to be passed over when positions become available. He asks a few of his colleagues for their thoughts on why he is not getting promoted, and he learns that others do not take him seriously. They share that he "clowns around" and is sarcastic and that some people don't know how to read him. He did not realize how much his sense of humor was interfering with his overall presentation and negatively impacting his progress on his goals. With this awareness, he can now work to make changes in his behavior and thus move closer to his ultimate goal. He grows his thought-feeling-behavior connections and becomes more skilled at managing his emotions and in interacting with others. Within months of making some key changes, he is promoted.

Self-Confidence

Don't let your ego get too close to your position, so that if your position gets shot down, your ego doesn't go with it.

—*Colin Powell*

Remember how you convinced the interviewer that you were the best person for the job? You are the best person, and she believes it, too! Show confidence as you take on the challenges of your new job. Being self-confident also enables you to take some risks—the risks that are a part of growing in your position or career.

Be ready to make mistakes, which is all part of the learning process. A good approach is to think positively and focus on positive thoughts. For example, "I will learn this," as opposed to, "I can't do this. I think I am in the wrong job." The second set of thoughts leads to feelings of helplessness, anxiety, and failure, which can lead to behaviors such as giving up or quitting.

Use your self-confidence to inspire and lead others. Show energy to pursue your goals, and show optimism despite setbacks. These emotions will spread to your staff.

EMOTIONAL INTELLIGENCE IN ACTION

Jeff is a mechanical engineer, recently promoted to a management position. His manager tells him that he will have to present his progress on an important project to key executives and the Board of Directors in one month. Jeff reflects on his emotions and realizes that he is anxious and dreading the presentation. He is aware that he is lacking self-confidence because he does not have strong presentation skills and does not enjoy being up in front of others. He wants to present himself and his information well but realizes he cannot expect to be a master presenter in four weeks! To increase his self-confidence, he decides to make improvements on his presentation skills. First, he develops an outline and a good PowerPoint presentation and practices his presentation in front of a mirror. He makes some changes in facial expressions and posture as well as voice tone based on what he sees and hears. He enlists his wife to listen to his presentation and asks her for honest feedback. She suggests that he smile more often and use his great sense of humor. He incorporates this into his presentation and practices again. He feels more confident about his presentation skills and chooses to maintain a positive attitude that he can and will present well. Jeff makes his presentation, and overall he feels he did an acceptable job. But he is relieved it is over. He knows this was an achievement for himself, and he hopes that it will be a little easier the next time he is asked to present.

Self-Management and Career Success

As you remember from Chapter 4, self-management consists of the following skills:

- Emotional self-control and adaptability
- Stress management
- Motivation and optimism

All of these skills will be useful on your new job.

Emotional Self-Control and Adaptability

Develop success from failures. Discouragement and failure are two of the surest stepping stones to success.

—*Dale Carnegie*

Use your EQ thought-feeling-behavior connections and manage your emotions. For example, you might be frustrated with yourself and need to use positive self-talk such as "Remember patience. This takes practice. I will become competent at this new task." Reflect on the thoughts you tell yourself, and expect some mistakes as you get started. Seek to learn from others.

Adapt yourself slowly to the situation and to new job responsibilities. Thoughts such as, "Change is good," and "Let's try this and see what happens," will lead to more positive feelings and adaptable behavior.

Remember that your coworkers are making their first impressions of you. How do you want to be viewed? Reflect on your behavior each day and decide what works well and what does not. Make changes by focusing on small steps first. If you want to be more flexible and adaptable, practice brainstorming possible approaches or ways to resolve a situation. Stop yourself from automatically choosing the path that you always take, and consider whether a different approach might work better.

EMOTIONAL INTELLIGENCE IN ACTION

Xavier is a salesman for an office supplies wholesaler who calls upon customers on a daily basis. His company starts an incentive program to increase sales, and the top prize is a Chevrolet Corvette convertible. Xavier adapts to the challenge and starts coming into work early and staying after hours, which cuts into his personal and fun time. To increase his customer base and sales, he also begins calling on customers with whom he has had a rocky relationship in the past. He has two good friends who work with him and also want the top prize. They go out on the weekends together and make a pact that they will keep their emotions in check and not let this sales incentive program interfere with their friendships outside of work. Despite Xavier's self-control, adaptability, and hard work, one of his friends wins the top prize and is awarded the Corvette. Xavier is greatly disappointed, but congratulates his friend. The good news is that he will have plenty of opportunities to at least ride in it!

Stress Management

Change is inevitable—except from a vending machine.

—Robert C. Gallagher

Starting a new job and learning new responsibilities is stressful, and everyone deals with stress in different ways. How do you deal with stress? Do you busy yourself with meaningless tasks? Do you shut down and fail to take any action? Do you dig in your heels and fight the change? Do you become very bossy and insist that others do things your way?

Looking at your thought-feeling-behavior connections can help you become aware of how stressors affect you. Once you are aware, you decide how to make a change to reduce your stress or to manage it. If you make yourself busy, take time to reflect on what your priorities are and take some simple steps in that direction. If you withdraw, resist and move towards a decision and focus on what to do to keep the process moving. If you find that you are resisting change, tell yourself that it is important to embrace and work with the change and use your energy positively. Share your ideas and be open to others' ideas. If you find yourself becoming too bossy, stop and allow others to speak and listen. Focus on what is most important in the situation at hand.

When you are stressed, have you ever noticed it is more difficult to manage your emotions? You have less energy to step back and reflect on how you are feeling. Reducing overall stress will naturally help you manage your emotions more effectively, especially the negative emotions of anger, frustration, and impatience.

Stress also affects your perceptions and your ability to accurately assess reality. It affects your readiness to deal with data as it comes to you. You feel overwhelmed and lack energy and thus do not process information as well or as accurately. You might spend less time brainstorming options and thus be less likely to make the best choice. To combat these side effects of stress, decide on how you will manage stress in your life on a day-to-day basis and stick with it.

Motivation and Optimism

Whether you think you can or you think you can't, you're right.

—*Henry Ford*

Staying motivated over time in your job is important because motivation drives your continued success. If you are motivated by advancement, you will work to exceed job requirements and expectations quickly to move onto the next level. If you are motivated by financial bonuses, you will work hard to exceed the set objectives to achieve your bonus. If you lose your motivation, it will affect your performance. Sometimes this is the signal that it is time to move on to another job or career. Use your self-awareness to stay alert to what is important to you in your job, and monitor it.

As I have mentioned throughout this book, optimism and a positive attitude go a long way in today's changing workforce. Positive thoughts lead to positive feelings and actions. You will face many challenges in your new job, from the pace of the work to the amount of work to be done. If you rise to the challenge and stay positive, you will be ahead of all those who don't. With continuing reorganizations, those employees who are negative and not adapting are at risk of going out the door.

During her performance review, her manager tells her that she is not performing to his or to the company standards and that she needs to make some changes. Upon reflection, she realizes that she is not motivated in this position. She is not using her strengths and not doing the work she loves and is thus not successful in achieving results. She talks with her manager, and they both agree that she should network in the company to find another position that more closely suits her interests and strengths.

You cannot change the reality of a situation, but you can change your attitude toward the reality. Your attitude is a combination of your thoughts and your feelings, and this combination affects behavior. *Optimism* is an attitude in which you choose to approach a situation in a positive way. Approaching a situation in a positive way sets you in a forward motion. In contrast, *pessimism* is an attitude in which you choose to approach the situation in a negative way. Remember from the earlier chapters how negative thoughts produce negative feelings. This can drain your energy and lead to unproductive behaviors, moving you in a direction away from your goal.

Social Awareness and Career Success

As you remember from Chapter 5, social awareness consists of the following skills:

- Empathy

- Reality testing

- Social responsibility

All of these skills will be useful on your new job.

Empathy

How far you go in life depends on your being tender with the young, compassionate with the aged, sympathetic with the striving, and tolerant of the weak and the strong—because someday you will have been all of these.

—George Washington Carver

Developing relationships with coworkers improves interactions and teamwork, and empathy is at the core of developing good relationships. Getting to know your coworkers on a personal basis will help you understand and respect how they work and what they value. In doing this, you establish a base upon which the relationship can grow both personally and professionally.

Work to understand others and their perspectives, and embrace individual differences. Remember that opportunities come from differences. Looking at an issue from multiple perspectives provides more information to assess a situation, which results in richer problem solving.

Empathy is critical to being a good manager and leader. Use your empathy to make positive connections, establish likeability, and develop solid working relationships. Employees perform best when they feel understood and valued for who they are and what they do. (Remember the exercise on likeable bosses from Chapter 1?)

EMOTIONAL INTELLIGENCE IN ACTION

Latrice is in charge of two diverse groups that eventually need to become one unit. She has been a member of one of the groups for years and is new to most of the people in the other group. Both groups are happy with things as they are and do not want to be combined for many reasons. Looking from each group's perspective, Latrice thinks about how she would feel in the situation and what would help her to transition if she were a group member. She then starts to spend more time with people from the group that she does not know and gets to know them and their concerns. She makes an effort to continue to connect one-on-one with the group she has been a part of but asks each member for his or her support and understanding on the demands of her time and attention. In addition, she asks them to step up and take the lead while she is working with the other team, stroking their experience and accountability and commitment. Latrice's empathy allows her to maneuver well to develop and maintain relationships with both groups and eventually bring them together.

Reality Testing

It's a recession when your neighbor loses his job; it is a depression when you lose yours.

—Harry S. Truman

The key to developing an accurate picture of your work situation, including how others perceive you and your job performance, is to gather information. This information can reaffirm your thoughts or add some new ideas to consider.

Performance evaluations and 360 assessments are formal ways of obtaining this information. In a more informal way, you can ask colleagues for feedback or seek out a mentor. A *mentor* is someone whom you can confide in and who has an interest in developing you. This can be someone within the company, possibly at a higher level, or a past colleague in another organization or industry. A mentor should be someone other than a family member or friend because these individuals cannot be fully objective or critical in their feedback. In order for this feedback to lead to change, you have to be ready to be honest and face what you might be doing that is keeping you from achieving your goals. You also have to have the motivation to improve.

If you are not sure you are reading a situation accurately, check it out by talking with others. Remember the thought-feeling-behavior connections and the importance of challenging thoughts and assumptions to be more realistic. In the book *The 7 Habits of Highly Effective People,* author Steven Covey talks about the habit "Seek first to understand, then to be understood." This habit entails really listening to others and understanding their perspective, as well as looking at the social setting and interpreting the data accurately. You want to avoid jumping to conclusions and putting in your preconceived notions of what might be going on. Gather information. Reflect on possibilities. Gather more information to verify your ideas and plans.

EMOTIONAL INTELLIGENCE IN ACTION

Pablo continues to be left out of meeting notices for a new department that he has started working with. He talks with the coordinator about not being informed of the recent meetings, and she places his name on the list. He receives meeting notices for a couple of weeks and then finds he is off the list again. At the same time, he starts thinking about the recent disagreements he has had with the top manager in those meetings. He starts to wonder if maybe he is being left off the notice list intentionally. Instead of assuming that this is the case, he goes back to the coordinator and asks about being left off the meeting notices. The coordinator looks into the situation and discovers that while she was on vacation, her substitute used an old meeting notice list

(continued)

(continued)

that did not include Pablo. She apologizes to him and then adds his name and rechecks the list. What would have happened if, instead of checking out the reality of the situation, Pablo had assumed the manager was intentionally leaving him out? He might have reacted by saying something to the manager in the meeting or by being less cooperative, which in the long run could be harmful to working relationships and not in line with the business at hand.

Social Responsibility

It's easy to make a buck. It's a lot tougher to make a difference.

—Tom Brokaw

When you work for a company, you are one of a group of people. Research shows that, with any group, certain group dynamics come into play. Be aware of the dynamics and use this knowledge to guide you in your interactions on the job.

One of the main dynamics is that a group develops norms or rules to follow. Sometimes these rules are spoken, and sometimes they are unspoken. One unspoken rule that your group at work might have is to arrive 15 minutes early to work. If you understand what the group rules are and how they affect your role or position, you can then develop a plan for managing yourself best in your position.

Another dynamic is the struggle for power and leadership in a group. Someone will step up to lead, and often another person challenges or competes for the spot. This is where politics comes into play in organizations. According to *Webster's New World Dictionary and Thesaurus*, *politics* is "the science and art of government" and "the factual scheming for power." As each group develops, there is a play for power and leadership. Understanding which people want leadership and how they influence you and your position is very important in succeeding in that organization.

Be aware that there are also different leadership roles. One person may be seen as the formal leader because he has the title and leads the meetings, but the group also might have an informal leader. An informal leader is someone who group members have come to perceive as important to the group and possibly as having expertise.

In a group, there is also the dynamic of independence versus dependence. You are a part of the group, and you interact with your group to achieve organizational goals. In addition, you act independently to do your particular role or job. You learn to balance this through awareness and social skills. If you are too independent, you might be seen as a loner by others. You might not have the alliances and relationships built to assist you when a problem does arise in which you need group support or assistance. However, aligning yourself with the wrong people can be equally detrimental to your job and career. For example, if you align with people who actively defy the leaders, the leaders will associate you with the rebels. You can then lose the support and influence of the leaders.

When you begin a new position, it is smart to be friendly and develop good working relationships with everyone. With time, you will learn and understand the group dynamics and the politics at play and decide how you are going to manage yourself and your job with this awareness.

Social responsibility is about commitment to the team and organization. Teamwork is critical to businesses today, and large amounts of money are spent on helping teams communicate and interact effectively. If you cannot be a team player, your work performance will suffer.

Being socially responsible is keeping your individual goals in line with your team and company goals. If your goals are in line, both you and the company win. The company profits from your alignment and from your productivity. Hopefully, in turn, you will be recognized by the company for the results that you achieve and the value you add. This recognition may lead to promotions and salary increases.

Social responsibility can extend beyond recognizing your role on a team, in a department, and in a company to being aware of your company's role in the industry, the community, and the world. Having this knowledge can aid you in developing improved processes, procedures, and products. Social awareness and responsibility can lead to making major changes in the business in order to impact the environment or community in helpful and positive ways.

EMOTIONAL INTELLIGENCE IN ACTION

Emily is an environmental engineer who works for an international company. She was attracted to the company due to its social awareness and responsibility to the community. However, as she climbs the management ladder, she

(continued)

(continued)

realizes that the direction the company wants to move in is not, in her view, the "right" direction for many reasons. She shares her concerns and suggests some new avenues in talking with her colleagues. However, she does not seek out anyone in upper management with whom she could address her concerns. She becomes unhappy in her position, feeling less influential, less valued, and more conflicted about where she is going and where the company is headed. She decides to start looking for another job in another company.

The problem here is that Emily doesn't step back to realize the politics involved and doesn't access influence from those above her. If she had met with an upper manager, she might have received the support. But she becomes frustrated and leaves the company instead of identifying and interacting within it. A better awareness of group dynamics and understanding of the importance of getting the support of leadership might have helped her.

Social Skills and Career Success

As you remember from Chapter 6, social skills include the following:

- Honesty, integrity, and trust
- Communication and assertiveness
- Cooperation, collaboration, and teamwork
- Conflict management and negotiation
- Influence on and development of others

All of these skills will be useful on your new job.

Honesty, Integrity, and Trust (H.I.T.)

Man cannot do right in one department of life whilst he is occupied in doing wrong in another department. Life is one indivisible whole.

—Ghandi

Just as you should radiate honesty in an interview, you also should show it every day in your interactions at work. Others then decide how much they can confide in and trust you. When you follow through on your commitments and keep your promises, you show that you are trustworthy.

People will not follow someone whom they do not trust. Trustworthiness is a basic quality needed in a leader. When leaders do what they say they are going to do, you come to believe in them and count on them. This is *credibility*.

> ### EMOTIONAL INTELLIGENCE IN ACTION
>
> Charlie is the manager of six sales representatives. Everyone on his team knows who the top two reps are with regard to sales and that these two reps seem to get a lot of extra perks. When one of the other sales reps on the team, Steve, questions Charlie about all of the extras that the top two reps are getting, Charlie says he has no control over that. He states that the perks are coming from the companies that those two particular reps call upon. However, later at a sales conference, Steve learns from an executive at one of those companies that the perks were given to Charlie by a different company altogether and that he could use them in whatever way he wanted to. Steve now distrusts his boss and tells the other team members, who in turn do not trust Charlie either. The team becomes more divided and mistrusting, which affects their job satisfaction and performance. Charlie has indeed set this stage through his dishonesty.

Communication and Assertiveness

I don't know the key to success, but the key to failure is trying to please everybody.

—*Bill Cosby*

Emotionally intelligent people are good communicators. They are in tune with themselves and how they impact others, and they are able to respond in ways to make a good connection.

Daily communication, both direct—in person—and indirect—through e-mail messages or phone calls—is important on the job. Daily communication keeps everyone working together and leads to better understanding of everyone's roles. Communicating expectations is important to smooth operations and needs to be carried out at all levels: upward to your manager; downward to those who report to you; and laterally to coworkers and peers, vendors, and clients.

When you communicate, you need to send and receive information. In a meeting, for example, you will need to decide when to listen and when to communicate your views. Being emotionally intelligent is being aware of the process and yourself and deciding how you want to influence and impact the group at that time.

When you do send messages, be an assertive communicator and express views with confidence and in a way that is respectful to others. In order for your conversation to go well, you not only want to deliver your message, but you also want your listeners to receive it well. So choose a time that works for them. In this way, they can be more open and receptive. Trying to talk with someone who is packing up her bags, putting on her coat, and telling you that she has to get home is not a good time to bring up your concerns. This is not being emotionally intelligent. When you are not sure about timing, ask permission first by saying, "Is now an acceptable time to ask you a question?" Or ask, "May we set up a time to talk about a couple of things?"

Identifying when others are taking advantage of you or when they are making unreasonable demands on you is part of assertiveness. Suppose your workload becomes overwhelming because you have had to take on a task of a coworker who left the company. Being assertive is talking to your manager and discussing what the priorities are and asking for direction. In this way, you are taking care of yourself, keeping your manager informed, listening to his concerns and expectations, and hopefully moving ahead with an agreeable solution. How many EQ skills can you identify in the past sentence? There are quite a few.

Emotionally intelligent managers communicate clearly and provide regular feedback. When a problem is identified, managers have to step up, suggest changes, and communicate what needs to be done. They need to act confidently and with initiative. They assess a situation (reality testing), develop a good understanding of their employees' perspectives and the situation (empathy), and then clearly communicate their concerns and directives. And emotionally intelligent managers do all of this in a way that shows they value employees and their positions.

EMOTIONAL INTELLIGENCE IN ACTION

Stefan knows that one of his direct reports is very unhappy about the way a decision came down from the corporate office. He values this employee and does not want to see her leave the company due to her dissatisfaction with this decision. Stefan believes it is important to talk with her about this corporate decision and allow her to express herself. In doing this, Stefan's goal is to show support, validate the employee's feelings and concerns, and assess what further steps can be taken. Stefan acts with emotional intelligence in that he wants to support the employee even though he might not be able to influence the situation. The relationship is stronger as a result of the communication.

EQ EXERCISE: IMPROVE COMMUNICATION ON THE JOB

Consider your communication with individuals at the following levels and think about how you can improve it.

Manager:_____

How often do I communicate with this person?_____

What kind of information do I communicate?_____

_____

How can I make the communication more effective?_____

_____

_____

When will I make this change?_____

Direct report:_____

How often do I communicate with this person?_____

What kind of information do I communicate?_____

_____

How can I make the communication more effective?_____

_____

_____

When will I make this change?_____

Peer:_____

How often do I communicate with this person?_____

What kind of information do I communicate?_____

_____

How can I make the communication more effective?_____

_____

_____

(continued)

(continued)

When will I make this change?_____

Customer:_____

How often do I communicate with this person?_____

What kind of information do I communicate?_____

_____

How can I make the communication more effective?_____

_____

_____

When will I make this change?_____

Cooperation, Collaboration, and Teamwork

I find the great thing in this world is not so much where we stand as in what direction we are moving.

—Oliver Wendell Holmes

Cooperation, collaboration, and teamwork are all about being other-centered instead of self-centered. Cooperation and collaboration work best when each member on a team is able to recognize and value others for their strengths and contributions. Acting in this way builds stronger cooperation and collaboration in the group. For example, group members often have difficulty accepting someone who has the view that he is the "smartest person in the room." Team members might actually work against this person instead of evaluating his ideas objectively. If you are emotionally intelligent, you are self-aware and would not allow yourself to fall into this role. Team members accept those who are confident and who speak up and share good ideas but who also listen and accept others' ideas.

EMOTIONAL INTELLIGENCE IN ACTION

Hannah and Vicki have very different work styles. Hannah likes to start on projects early and finish ahead of the deadline. If she is not able to do this, she feels nervous that the project won't get done on time. She becomes impatient with others who hold up her progress. Vicki, on the other hand, has always been more laid back. She gets things done but works best with a pending deadline. She likes the pressure it creates, and she feels she works best in these situations. Hannah and Vicki have to work together on a project, so they discuss their different work styles and try to figure out how they can respect one another's styles but still get the project completed on time. Hannah suggests that she gather and compile the information and turn it over to Vicki a week before the deadline. Vicki commits to completing the report and reassures Hannah that she will make the deadline.

EQ EXERCISE: RECOGNIZE THE STRENGTHS OF OTHERS

How much do you recognize others for a job well done? Think of coworkers in the following roles, and note the strengths that you admire about them. Do you share this with them?

Manager:_____

Strengths I admire:_____

How and when can I communicate my recognition and appreciation to this person?_____

_____

Direct report:_____

Strengths I admire:_____

How and when can I communicate my recognition and appreciation to this person?_____

_____

Peer:_____

Strengths I admire:_____

How and when can I communicate my recognition and appreciation to this person? _____

_____

(continued)

(continued)

> **Customer:**_____
>
> Strengths I admire:_____
>
> How and when can I communicate my recognition and appreciation
> to this person?_____
>
> _____

Conflict Management and Negotiation

The road to success is always under construction.

—Arnold Palmer

Conflict management and negotiation are EQ skills that you will need on
occasion. To use these skills successfully, you first need to develop good
working relationships.

Dealing with conflict sometimes takes a high level of a communication
skill called confrontation. *Confrontation* is talking to others when they
do not live up to the agreed-upon expectations or when they display a
behavior that does not fit in with the values and goals of the company.
Confrontation is the process of holding people accountable and addressing
the consequences that result when people stray from the desired course. To
effectively confront others on their actions requires the EQ skills of self-
confidence and assertiveness. You have to believe you are acting correctly
and for good reasons when you confront someone. The goal is to point
out and encourage the individual to change the behavior, which will help
develop the person and bring him or her into alignment with the team and
company goals. The confrontation should not be made for your personal
benefit but in service of the group and organizational goals.

The skill of negotiation is needed when team members disagree. *Negotiation* means there are opposing interests and sides that have to come to some
common ground or agreement to bring completion to a task or situation.
Negotiation skills are built upon the other basic social skills mentioned
previously: honest and assertive communication and a spirit of cooperation
and collaboration. All of these skills are necessary to conduct a successful
negotiation and thus resolve the conflict. Always keep in mind that any

work-related negotiation involves a larger and common issue: how best to serve the goals of the company.

> ## EMOTIONAL INTELLIGENCE IN ACTION
>
> Tariq and Karen are both vice presidents in charge of different departments of the same company. Although there is a great deal of competition between them, they also maintain a professional attitude and respect for each other in their positions. Each quarter they have to decide how to present a state of the company address to the company's 300 employees and who is going to present what information. Each time they differ on what and how information will be shared, and completing the presentation entails lengthy discussions and a great deal of negotiation and compromise. They both know it and accept this going into their preparation meeting. Tariq shares what he wants to do and supports it and listens to Karen as she does the same, and vice versa. They often "agree to disagree." They have to give and take in order to reach an agreement. Neither of them will get all that they want; the final presentation is always a compromise. Yet Tariq and Karen realize that they want to maintain their good working rapport and accept and resolve their differences for the good of the company (social responsibility).

Influence on and Development of Others

Take care of those who work for you, and you'll float to greatness on their achievements.

—H.S.M. Burns

Developing others is a skill utilized by a leader, manager, teacher, coach, or mentor with the ultimate goal of helping others reach their personal and professional goals. Developing others involves being able to recognize strengths and encourage employees in their roles in the organization. The ability to identify each employee's strengths and then develop those strengths to be utilized to the fullest in achieving the company's goals and producing results is what organizational development is all about. An emotionally intelligent person knows when to support, when to challenge, and when to confront in the service of the organization. They can use all aspects of their EQ.

Developing others entails the skill of delegation. You are making a decision when to do a task yourself and when to teach others to do it. Developing others also entails motivating others to achieve. The process of instilling hope and faith in someone while giving them the tools to achieve a task allows them to grow and advance. The more you are able to grow and advance others, the better leader you are.

I recently saw Jack Welch, Chairman and CEO of GE from 1981 to 2001, give a presentation. The audience asked him numerous questions, and one of his answers in particular has stayed with me because it makes such good, valuable sense. Someone asked, "What one thing truly makes a leader successful?" He shared that a successful leader is "turned on by the success of his people and their growth." He explained that a leader is able to differentiate the strong performers from the weak ones and uses this information. A successful leader is also "generous in spirit and revels in team success."

EMOTIONAL INTELLIGENCE IN ACTION

I worked with a boss who was very skilled at influencing and developing her staff to bring about good business results. She was manager of a team of school-based social workers, and she enjoyed her position and did well in it. What stood out to me was her ability to understand the needs of her staff and address those needs in creative ways. In doing this, she enabled and empowered her staff to do their jobs effectively and meet their requirements.

For example, the team members worked at different school sites across the city during the week, and then met altogether for meetings and paperwork on Fridays. Friday meetings were the medium for sharing the latest changes in paperwork or delivery of services that had been passed down by management. You can understand that Fridays were not always viewed in such a positive light.

My boss, showing her understanding of staff needs, decided to shape Fridays into more positive days. Her goal was to bring unity amongst a diverse staff that only came together for a couple of hours a week and to create an environment that was welcoming and fun in order to support staff as they dealt with the ongoing stress of their jobs. She brought food in to weekly staff meetings and encouraged personal sharing each week. Over time, others joined in to bring food, and there was more personal sharing outside of the meetings. Birthdays and individual accomplishments were recognized by the team. Staff supported one another as each grumbled about their latest concerns or tackled the newest changes in paperwork. My boss created an atmosphere where staff could state their concerns openly, but she stepped up when the discussion was over to communicate the final decision and expectations.

EQ EXERCISE: FOCUS ON EQ SKILLS IN YOUR NEW JOB

Choose skills that you want to focus on developing in your new job and list action steps that you plan to take to improve these skills. Think ahead and list possible obstacles you might encounter and ways to get around them if they should arise.

Skill:_____

Action steps:_____

_____

_____

Potential obstacles:_____

_____

Ways to overcome obstacles:_____

_____

_____

Evaluate progress on this date:_____

Skill:_____

Action steps:_____

_____

Potential obstacles:_____

_____

Ways to overcome obstacles:_____

_____

_____

Evaluate progress on this date:_____

Chapter Reflections

To be the most successful in your new job, use and continue to develop your EQ. Identify your emotions as you interact with others, which will give you information on how to best handle the situation. Remember, your emotional state affects others. If you are happy and positive, this will spread to others around you and they will pick up on those positive feelings. If you are angry, this will spread in much the same way. Keep tabs on your emotions as well as on your performance. Once you have the job, continue to assess what you are doing well and what you need to improve. Showing confidence and a positive attitude will help you get through the challenges of a new job.

Managing your emotions will improve your work performance and develop good connections with others. Expect some mistakes as you get started, because this is part of learning a new job. Seek to learn from others. Show your flexibility and try to adapt to the new situation. Monitor your motivation and take positive steps to effectively manage your stress on and off the job.

You are learning your new responsibilities and tasks, but at the same time you are developing relationships with your coworkers and boss. Identifying the company culture and values as well as the organizational dynamics and using this knowledge in your interactions can move you further towards your goal.

Emotionally intelligent people are in tune with themselves and how they impact others. They can read others and the situation well, understand how they are affected by others' emotions and behaviors, and can respond accordingly. As a manager or leader, using your EQ skills will mold productive and effective employees and teams, which will produce good business results and grow an emotionally intelligent organization.

References

Auerbach, Jeffrey E. *Personal and Executive Coaching: The Complete Guide for Mental Health Professionals.* New York, NY: Executive College Press, 2001.

Ballou, Mary. *Psychological Interventions: A Guide to Strategies.* Westport, CT: Praeger, 1995.

Bar-On, Reuven. *EQ-i Bar-On Emotional Quotient Inventory: A Measure of Emotional Intelligence, Technical Manual.* Toronto, ON: Multi-Health Systems, Inc., 1997.

Beck, Aaron. *Cognitive Therapy of Depression.* New York, NY: Guilford, 1979.

Birkman, Roger. *True Colors: Get to Know Yourself and Others Better with the Highly Acclaimed Birkman Method.* Nashville, TN: Thomas Nelson, Inc., 1995.

Bolles, Richard Nelson. *What Color Is Your Parachute? 1999: A Practical Manual for Job-Hunters and Career-Changers.* New York, NY: Ten Speed Press, 1999.

Bolles, Richard Nelson. *What Color Is Your Parachute? 2009: A Practical Manual for Job-Hunters and Career-Changers.* New York, NY: Ten Speed Press, 2009.

Burns, David. *Feeling Good: The New Mood Therapy.* New York, NY: Collins, 1980.

College of Executive Coaching. *Personal and Executive Coach Training Program.* Pismo Beach, CA, 2000–2004.

Consortium for Research on Emotional Intelligence in Organizations. *Emotional Intelligence.* http://www.eiconsortium.org.

Covey, Stephen R. *The Seven Habits of Highly Effective People: Restoring the Character Ethic.* New York, NY: Simon and Schuster, 1989.

Ellis, Albert. *Reason and Emotion in Psychotherapy.* Secaucus, NJ: Carol Pub. Group, 1994.

Franklin, Donald J. "Cognitive Therapy for Depression." *Psychology Information Online.* http://www.psychologyinfo.com/depression/cognitive.htm (accessed April 15, 2009).

Freedman, Joshua, and Todd Everett. *White Paper: The Business Case for Emotional Intelligence.* Six Seconds, 2008.

Funny Quotes. *AmusingQuotes.com.* http://www.amusingquotes.com (accessed July 20, 2009).

Gardner, Howard. *Frames of Mind: The Theory of Multiple Intelligences.* New York, NY: Basic Books, 1983.

Goleman, Daniel. *Emotional Intelligence: Why It Can Matter More Than IQ.* New York, NY: Bantam, 1997.

Goleman, Daniel. *Social Intelligence: The New Science of Human Relationships.* New York, NY: Bantam, 2006.

Goleman, Daniel. "What Makes a Leader?" *Harvard Business Review* (November–December 1998).

Goleman, Daniel. *Working with Emotional Intelligence.* New York, NY: Bantam, 1998.

Goleman, Daniel, Annie McKee, and Richard E. Boyatzis. *Primal Leadership: Realizing the Power of Emotional Intelligence.* Boston, MA: Harvard Business School Press, 2002.

Hall, Doug. *Jump Start Your Business Brain: Win More, Lose Less, and Make More Money with Your New Products, Services, Sales and Advertising.* Cincinnati, OH: Brain Brew Books, 2001.

Hayes, Steven J. *Basic Quotations.* http://www.basicquotations.com (accessed July 20, 2009).

Jankowski, Katherine. *The Job Seeker's Guide to Socially Responsible Companies.* Detroit, MI: Visible Ink Press, 1995.

Kelly, Matthew. *The Book of Courage.* Cincinnati, OH: Beacon Publishing, 2003.

Kelly, Matthew. *Rediscovering Catholicism: Journeying Toward Our Spiritual North Star.* Huntington, IN: Our Sunday Visitor, 2003.

LinkedIn Corporation. *LinkedIn.* http://www.linkedin.com.

Lynn, Adele B. *The EQ Difference: A Powerful Plan for Putting Emotional Intelligence to Work.* New York, NY: AMACOM/American Management Association, 2004.

Lynn, Adele B. *The EQ Interview: Finding Employees with High Emotional Intelligence.* New York, NY: AMACOM / American Management Association, 2008.

Maslow, A.H. "A Theory of Human Motivation," *Psychological Review,* 50, 370–396.

McKay, Matthew, Martha Davis, and Patrick Fanning. *Messages: The Communication Skills Book.* Minneapolis, MN: New Harbinger Publications, 1995.

Multi-Health Systems, Inc. *EI Insider Report Newsletter,* May 2009. http://www.mhs.com.

Multi-Health Systems, Inc. *Emotional Quotient Inventory (EQ-i): A Training and Certification Workshop.* 2001.

Myers, Isabel. *Introduction to TYPE: A Guide to Understanding Your Results on the Myers-Briggs Type Indicator.* Mountain View, CA: CPP, Inc., 1998.

NETability. *Job-Hunt.* http://www.job-hunt.org.

*O*NET Dictionary of Occupational Titles,* Fourth Edition. Indianapolis, IN: JIST Publishing, 2007. Online: http://online.onetcenter.org.

PAQ Services, Inc. *SalaryExpert.* http://www.salaryexpert.com.

Salary.com, Inc. *Salary.com.* http://www.salary.com.

Salovey, Peter, and David J. Sluyter, editors. *Emotional Development and Emotional Intelligence: Educational Implications.* New York, NY: Basic Books, 1997.

Seligman, Martin E.P. *Learned Optimism: How to Change Your Mind and Your Life.* New York, NY: Vintage, 2006.

Stanton, Sandra Sunquist. Seminar: *Brain Coaching: Tapping Body and Spirit to Max the Mind.* Connections of the Heart, LLC, and Health Ed Network, 2008.

Stein, Steven J., and Howard E. Book. *The EQ Edge: Emotional Intelligence and Your Success.* Toronto, ON: Stoddart, 2002.

U.S. Department of Labor. *Occupational Outlook Handbook 2008–2009.* Indianapolis, IN: JIST Publishing, 2008. Online: http://www.bls.gov/oco.

Webster's New World Dictionary and Thesaurus. New York, NY: Hungry Minds, Inc., 2002.

INDEX

K–L

M–N

O